HOW TO PLAY
BETTER SCRABBLE®

Darryl Francis

Chambers

Scrabble® is a registered trademark owned in the USA
and Canada by Milton Bradley Company, Massachusetts,
and elsewhere by J W Spear and Sons PLC,
Enfield, Middlesex EN3 7TB, UK

CHAMBERS
An imprint of Larousse plc,
43–45 Annandale Street, Edinburgh EH7 4AZ

First published by Chambers 1994
10 9 8 7 6 5 4 3 2 1

A CIP catalogue for this book
is available from the British Library

ISBN 0 550 19029 5

Typeset by Hewer Text Composition Services, Edinburgh
Printed in England by Clays Ltd, St Ives plc

Contents

Contents

Contents

1

Introduction

This book is aimed at several different sorts of Scrabble player. It is aimed at the learner player who is still trying to master the rules of the game. It is aimed at the player who wants to improve their social game, probably played with family or friends. This player has already mastered the basic rules, but wants to achieve higher scores and improve their winning abilities. The book is aimed at the club player who has already picked up many of the techniques for playing better Scrabble, but has never been presented with a systematic approach to playing the game better.

Unlike in most other books about Scrabble, considerable attention is paid here to the two very different kinds of Scrabble that can be played – playing for high scores and playing to win. The different techniques necessary for playing these styles of the game are explained fully in the book.

Much emphasis is placed on the need to have an extensive armoury of words useful for Scrabble. If you want to add words to your armoury, this book tells you the ones to concentrate on. More about two-letter words, hooks and seven-letter anagrams later on!

Although the book is not aimed at the very top-level player, you should find sufficient in it to enable you to play at any of the organized Scrabble events and tournaments that are staged up and down the country – without disgracing yourself!

Author's notes:
> When writing a book about Scrabble, much use is made of numbers. Some numbers in this book are shown using figures (such as 5, 83, 200) and some are spelled out with words. If the mixed use of figures and words seems inconsistent to you, the reasoning behind the use is as follows. All letter tile values are

written as figures (for example, the K has a point value of 5 points); all scores are written as figures (for example, a 50-point bonus, her score was increased by 22 points, he scored 435 points). Large numbers are written using figures (for example, there are 100 tiles in a set, there are 200 words in a list). Words are used for counting things, especially where the number concerned is small (for example, a one-volume dictionary, a two-player game, six tiles on her rack, the seven-tile minimum, an eight-letter word). All illustrative diagrams (figures!) are referred to by figures (for example, Figure 35).

Although Scrabble seems to be played by more women than men, use of 'he or she' and 'his or her' has been avoided. Where a masculine pronoun has been used, the equivalent feminine pronoun is also implied.

2

The Basics

Introduction
This chapter explains the basics of Scrabble. What's the game about? What are the physical things that make up the game? And what are the rules for playing the game? How do you score? What happens if you can't make a word, or don't want to make one? What happens if you don't like the tiles you have?

Outline of the Game

Scrabble is a word-building game, which is usually played by two players, although it is possible to play with three, four or even more players. If you want to play Scrabble seriously or competitively, then it is definitely a two-player game. But if you want to play Scrabble for fun, or to while away a wet weekend afternoon, then you can have two or more players involved.

Each player has a number of letter tiles, each with a point value. The point values range from 1 point for an A to 10 points for a Z. The players take it in turn to make a word (or words) on a board composed of squares, by placing some or all of their letter tiles into the squares. Words played must connect with words already placed on the board, and words may be entirely new words or modifications of words already played. More about this later in the chapter. Players score points for the words made on each move. A player's score for an individual move will depend on the words made and the individual squares covered on the board. Play rotates amongst the players, each one having a turn, until all the letter tiles are used up. The winner is the player who has scored the highest total number of points.

The Hardware

The essential items in a Scrabble set (the hardware) are a board, 100 letter tiles, four racks, and a bag to keep the letter tiles in. A Scrabble set also comes with score-sheets, the rules of the game, and a list of some useful words. De luxe versions of the game also include a timer.

The Scrabble board is a grid with 15 rows and 15 columns, with a total of 225 squares. The columns are labelled A to O (from left to right), and the rows are labelled 1 to 15 (from top to bottom). In this way, the position of any square on the board can be accurately but briefly defined. For example, the square at the top left-hand corner is A1, the square at the top right-hand corner is O1, the square at the bottom left-hand corner is A15, the square at the bottom right-hand corner is O15, and the square at the centre of the board is H8. And so on. It would be helpful if you became familiar with these labels, because they will be used later in the book to define accurately a word's starting position on the board. It is much more precise to say that a word goes across from square B9 rather than to try and describe it in some long-winded way.

The squares on the board come in 5 different colours: grey, light blue, dark blue, pink and red. The four different sorts of coloured squares (that is, the non-grey ones) are called premium squares. Each of the coloured squares has an effect on the point value of the letter (and perhaps the word) covering a particular square. The premium squares are summarized here:

light blue	double letter score square	2L
dark blue	triple letter score square	3L
pink	double word score square	2W
red	triple word score square	3W

The effects of these different premium squares will be explained a little later in the section on scoring, although you can probably begin to guess at how they influence scores.

The premium squares are arranged symmetrically on the Scrabble board, with the left- and right-hand halves mirroring each other, and the top and bottom halves mirroring each other. Figure 1 shows a typical Scrabble board, with the premium squares shaded to represent colours, before any letter tiles have been placed on the board. Figure 2 shows a typical Scrabble board, with the premium squares marked 2L, 3L, 2W and 3W – again, before any letter tiles have been placed on it. It would be helpful if you became familiar with the 'shorthand' 2L, 3L, 2W and 3W as these will be used later in the book.

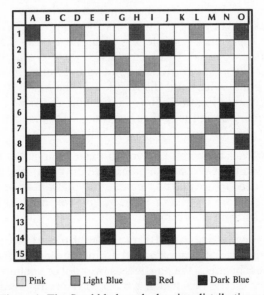

Pink | Light Blue | Red | Dark Blue

Figure 1: The Scrabble board, showing distribution of premium squares

	A	B	C	D	E	F	G	H	I	J	K	L	M	N	O
1	3W			2L				3W				2L			3W
2		2W				3L				3L				2W	
3			2W				2L		2L				2W		
4	2L			2W				2L				2W			2L
5					2W						2W				
6		3L				3L				3L				3L	
7			2L				2L		2L				2L		
8	3W			2L				2W				2L			3W
9			2L				2L		2L				2L		
10		3L				3L				3L				3L	
11					2W						2W				
12	2L			2W				2L				2W			2L
13			2W				2L		2L				2W		
14		2W				3L				3L				2W	
15	3W			2L				3W				2L			3W

Figure 2: The Scrabble board, showing distribution of premium squares, using the 2L, 3L, 2W and 3W notation

The standard English-language version of the game has 100 letter tiles – 98 of which show letters and point values, and two of which are blanks. Some letters occur more times than other letters. For example, there are 12 E's, three G's and one K. Different letters have different point values, ranging from 1 to 10. The point values and distribution of the letters and letter tiles is shown in Figure 3. Note that the blank has no (or zero) point value. Foreign-language versions of the game are available, but they do not all have 100 letter tiles.

The four racks are for players to keep their letter tiles on during a game. Of course, if there are only two players, you will only need to use two of the racks! If you want to organize a game with more than four players, you will need to borrow extra racks from another set.

The bag is used to hold all 100 of the letter tiles at the start of a game, with tiles being removed from the bag as the game progresses. In effect, the bag acts as the pool of unchosen letter tiles – that is, the tiles which have neither been played on the board nor are on the players' racks. The bag can also be used to store the tiles when the game equipment is put away.

Getting Started

As has already been pointed out, the number of players can be two or more. The first thing to do is to decide the order in which the players take their turns. This is done by each player choosing one tile from the bag, or pool, of unchosen letters. The player drawing a letter closest to the beginning of the alphabet starts.

In the case of two players, it is merely a question of this deciding which one has the first turn.

In the case of three players, the player whose tile was closest to the beginning of the alphabet has the first turn, and the player whose letter was second closest has the second turn. This effectively determines whether the order of play goes clockwise or anticlockwise.

In the case of four or more players, the player whose tile was closest to the beginning of the alphabet has the first turn, the player whose tile was second closest has the second turn, and so on. It is probably sensible for players to change their seats if necessary, in order to ensure that play always goes to the next player on the left (or right).

In selecting tiles, any player drawing a blank tile should return it to the bag and choose another tile. If two or more players draw the same letter, they should return these and pick tiles

Letter	Point value	Number of tiles
A	1	9
B	3	2
C	3	2
D	2	4
E	1	12
F	4	2
G	3	3
H	4	2
I	1	9
J	8	1
K	5	1
L	1	4
M	3	2
N	1	6
O	1	8
P	3	2
Q	10	1
R	1	6
S	1	4
T	1	6
U	1	4
V	4	2
W	4	2
X	8	1
Y	4	2
Z	10	1
blank	0	2

Figure 3: Point values and distribution of letter tiles

The Basics

afresh, ensuring that all players have different letters before the order of play is finally decided.

Once the playing order has been determined, all tiles should be returned to the bag, and shuffled well. In the order just determined, players should now take it in turn to draw seven tiles from the bag, without looking at them, and place them face up on their racks, ensuring that the other players cannot see the tiles. Once all players have seven tiles, the game is ready to get under way.

At least one of the players should be the designated score-keeper. The method of selecting the score-keeper is left to your own initiative! After the first game, players can either take it in turn to keep score or, alternatively, all players may wish to keep track of all the scores.

The First Play

At the centre of the Scrabble board, on square H8, is a pink square with a star in it. The rules stipulate that the first word played on the board must go through this central pink square. Because it is a pink square, it is effectively a double-word-score square, or a 2W square if you recall the shorthand!

The first player must use two or more of his tiles to form a word going through the central pink square. It doesn't have to start or finish on the pink square, although it may do. The word can be placed vertically (down column H) or horizontally (along row 8). Diagonal plays are never permitted! The player counts up the score for his word, announces it to the other players, and records the score on a score-sheet. How to count up the score and how to keep the score-sheet will be explained in detail a little later.

The first player now takes fresh tiles from the pool of unchosen ones, bringing the number of tiles on his rack back up to seven. Play now passes to the next player.

The Next Plays

The next player must now play one or more of his seven tiles on the board, creating a new word, or modifying the word already on the board. The tiles played must all be in the same row or column, and must interlock, crossword-fashion, with the word already on the board. The player scores points for the new words made, as well as for any word modified. His total score for the turn is the sum of the scores of the individual new and modified words. After announcing his score, the player selects sufficient tiles from the pool to bring the number on his rack back to seven.

Play now progresses in this way to all the players. The first player will eventually get a second turn, a third turn, and so on. Each player can play one or more of their tiles, making new words, modifying existing words, or both, adding up their scores, announcing their scores, and taking further tiles from the pool. Play continues to rotate among all the players until the end of the game is reached – more on this a little later.

Making Words
Figure 4 shows a possible first play, with the word RATE having been played on row 8, with the initial R on square E8. The same word could also have been played across beginning at F8, G8 and H8, or could have been played down beginning at H5, H6, H7 and H8.

A variety of moves which could build on RATE are offered here. They show the different ways in which letters can be added before, after and around RATE.

Words can be modified by the addition of a single letter in front of them. Figure 5 shows a possible subsequent play, turning RATE into GRATE, by the simple addition of the letter G on square D8. The player who put down just the G will score points for the whole word GRATE, though.

Words can be modified by the addition of a single letter after them. Figure 6 shows an alternative subsequent play, turning RATE into RATED, by the addition of the letter D on square I8. Similarly, the player who put down the D will score points for the whole word RATED.

Words may have two or more letters added in front of them. Figure 7 shows another subsequent play, turning RATE into AERATE, by the addition of AE on squares C8 and D8.

Words may have two or more letters added after them. Figure 8 shows RATE being turned into RATEABLE, with the addition of ABLE on squares I8, J8, K8 and L8.

Words may have letters added at both ends. Figure 9 shows how RATE could become NARRATED.

You don't have to modify an existing word, though. You might just choose to play an entirely new word, at right angles to a word already on the board. Figure 10 shows how the letter E of RATE is used to help make the new word CREEK. The player only scores points for CREEK, since RATE has not been modified.

A move could combine the playing of an entirely new word with the modification of an existing word. Figure 11 shows how CADDY could be played perpendicular to RATE, turning RATE into RATED at the same time. In this instance, the player scores points for both CADDY and RATED.

A move could involve playing several new words, by placing a word parallel with one or more letters of an existing word. Figure 12 shows how HOPE has been played, creating the vertical two-letter word HE at the same time. The player will score points for both HOPE and HE.

Figure 13 is an extension of the last example. The word TOKEN has been played parallel to RATE, with the vertical words RE and AN also being made. This move will score points for all three words: TOKEN, RE and AN.

Figure 14 takes the last example further still. The word VENOM is played parallel to RATE, creating four vertical words: RE, AN, TO and EM. Points are scored for all five words.

The maximum number of words that can be made or modified at one turn is eight – one entirely new word and seven perpendicular words. Figure 15 shows how the word SATIRES could be played parallel to ANIMATE, already on the board, thereby making seven two-letter words – AS, NA, IT, MI, AR, TE and ES. Don't worry if you don't recognize some of these two-letter words yet! Points would be scored for all eight of these words.

By now, you might be beginning to see the potential utility of two-letter words. But more about two-letter words later.

Figure 4: A first move of RATE, played from E8 across

Figure 5: Modifying RATE, to make GRATE

	A	B	C	D	E	F	G	H	I	J	K	L	M	N	O
1	3W			2L				3W				2L			3W
2		2W				3L				3L				2W	
3			2W				2L		2L				2W		
4	2L			2W				2L				2W			2L
5					2W						2W				
6		3L				3L				3L				3L	
7			2L				2L		2L				2L		
8	3W			2L	R	A	T	E	D			2L			3W
9			2L				2L		2L				2L		
10		3L				3L				3L				3L	
11				2W							2W				
12	2L			2W				2L				2W			2L
13			2W				2L		2L				2W		
14		2W				3L				3L				2W	
15	3W			2L				3W				2L			3W

Figure 6: Modifying RATE, to make RATED

	A	B	C	D	E	F	G	H	I	J	K	L	M	N	O
1	3W			2L				3W				2L			3W
2		2W				3L				3L				2W	
3			2W				2L		2L				2W		
4	2L			2W				2L				2W			2L
5					2W						2W				
6		3L				3L				3L				3L	
7			2L				2L		2L				2L		
8	3W		A	E	R	A	T	E				2L			3W
9			2L				2L		2L				2L		
10		3L				3L				3L				3L	
11				2W							2W				
12	2L			2W				2L				2W			2L
13			2W				2L		2L				2W		
14		2W				3L				3L				2W	
15	3W			2L				3W				2L			3W

Figure 7: Modifying RATE, to make AERATE

	A	B	C	D	E	F	G	H	I	J	K	L	M	N	O
1	3W			2L				3W				2L			3W
2		2W				3L				3L				2W	
3			2W				2L		2L				2W		
4	2L			2W				2L				2W			2L
5					2W						2W				
6		3L				3L				3L				3L	
7			2L				2L		2L				2L		
8	3W			2L	R	A	T	E	A	B	L	E			3W
9			2L				2L		2L				2L		
10		3L				3L				3L				3L	
11				2W							2W				
12	2L			2W				2L				2W			2L
13			2W				2L		2L				2W		
14		2W				3L				3L				2W	
15	3W			2L				3W				2L			3W

Figure 8: Modifying RATE, to make RATEABLE

	A	B	C	D	E	F	G	H	I	J	K	L	M	N	O
1	3W			2L				3W				2L			3W
2		2W				3L				3L				2W	
3			2W				2L		2L				2W		
4	2L			2W				2L				2W			2L
5					2W						2W				
6		3L				3L				3L				3L	
7			2L				2L		2L				2L		
8	3W	N	A	R	R	A	T	E	D			2L			3W
9			2L				2L		2L				2L		
10		3L				3L				3L				3L	
11				2W							2W				
12	2L			2W				2L				2W			2L
13			2W				2L		2L				2W		
14		2W				3L				3L				2W	
15	3W			2L				3W				2L			3W

Figure 9: Modifying RATE, to make NARRATED

	A	B	C	D	E	F	G	H	I	J	K	L	M	N	O
1	3W			2L				3W				2L			3W
2		2W				3L			3L					2W	
3			2W				2L		2L				2W		
4	2L			2W				2L				2W			2L
5					2W						2W				
6		3L				3L		C	3L					3L	
7			2L				2L	R	2L				2L		
8	3W			2L	R	A	T	E				2L			3W
9			2L				2L	E	2L				2L		
10		3L				3L		K	3L					3L	
11				2W							2W				
12	2L			2W				2L				2W			2L
13			2W				2L		2L				2W		
14		2W				3L			3L					2W	
15	3W			2L				3W				2L			3W

Figure 10: Using the E of RATE to make CREEK

	A	B	C	D	E	F	G	H	I	J	K	L	M	N	O
1	3W			2L				3W				2L			3W
2		2W				3L			3L					2W	
3			2W				2L		2L				2W		
4	2L			2W				2L				2W			2L
5				2W					C		2W				
6		3L				3L			A					3L	
7			2L				2L		D				2L		
8	3W			2L	R	A	T	E	D			2L			3W
9			2L				2L		Y				2L		
10		3L				3L			3L					3L	
11				2W							2W				
12	2L			2W				2L				2W			2L
13			2W				2L		2L				2W		
14		2W				3L			3L					2W	
15	3W			2L				3W				2L			3W

Figure 11: Playing CADDY, and modifying RATE, to make RATED

	A	B	C	D	E	F	G	H	I	J	K	L	M	N	O
1	3W			2L				3W				2L			3W
2		2W				3L				3L				2W	
3			2W				2L		2L				2W		
4	2L			2W				2L				2W			2L
5					2W						2W				
6		3L				3L				3L				3L	
7			2L				2L	H	O	P	E		2L		
8	3W			2L	R	A	T	E				2L			3W
9			2L				2L		2L				2L		
10		3L				3L				3L				3L	
11					2W						2W				
12	2L			2W				2L				2W			2L
13			2W				2L		2L				2W		
14		2W				3L				3L				2W	
15	3W			2L				3W				2L			3W

Figure 12: Playing HOPE, as well as HE

	A	B	C	D	E	F	G	H	I	J	K	L	M	N	O
1	3W			2L				3W				2L			3W
2		2W				3L				3L				2W	
3			2W				2L		2L				2W		
4	2L			2W				2L				2W			2L
5					2W						2W				
6		3L				3L				3L				3L	
7			2L				2L		2L				2L		
8	3W			2L	R	A	T	E				2L			3W
9		T	O	K	E	N	2L		2L				2L		
10		3L				3L				3L				3L	
11					2W						2W				
12	2L			2W				2L				2W			2L
13			2W				2L		2L				2W		
14		2W				3L				3L				2W	
15	3W			2L				3W				2L			3W

Figure 13: Playing TOKEN, as well as RE and AN

	A	B	C	D	E	F	G	H	I	J	K	L	M	N	O
1	3W			2L				3W				2L			3W
2		2W				3L				3L				2W	
3			2W				2L		2L				2W		
4	2L			2W				2L				2W			2L
5					2W						2W				
6		3L				3L				3L				3L	
7			2L				2L		2L				2L		
8	3W			2L	R	A	T	E				2L			3W
9			2L	V	E	N	O	M	2L				2L		
10		3L				3L				3L				3L	
11				2W							2W				
12	2L			2W				2L				2W			2L
13			2W				2L		2L				2W		
14		2W				3L				3L				2W	
15	3W			2L				3W				2L			3W

Figure 14: Playing VENOM, as well as RE, AN, TO and EM

	A	B	C	D	E	F	G	H	I	J	K	L	M	N	O
1	3W			2L				3W				2L			3W
2		2W				3L				3L				2W	
3			2W				2L		2L				2W		
4	2L			2W				2L				2W			2L
5					2W						2W				
6		3L				3L				3L				3L	
7			2L				2L		2L				2L		
8	3W	A	N	I	M	A	T	E				2L			3W
9		S	A	T	I	R	E	S	2L				2L		
10		3L				3L				3L				3L	
11				2W							2W				
12	2L			2W				2L				2W			2L
13			2W				2L		2L				2W		
14		2W				3L				3L				2W	
15	3W			2L				3W				2L			3W

Figure 15: Playing SATIRES, as well as AS, NA, IT, MI, AR, TE and ES

Scoring

The previous section described how words can be made and modified on the Scrabble board. But how do you work out the score for the word or words played at each player's turn? The combination of tile point values and premium squares covered needs to be understood.

First of all, you need to be clear about the words you have made in a particular move. Usually, only one or two words are made (or modified), so there isn't too much of a problem. But it is possible, occasionally, to play more words than this. Make sure you don't overlook any words that have been played. Even if you add a single letter to a word already on the board, thereby making another word, then you will score points for that newly-made word. For example, if the word ZOO was already on the board, and you added a solitary S to it, making the word ZOOS, you will score points for that whole word.

The score for each word needs to be added up, taking into account the effects of any premium squares that you have covered *on that move*. (Note the emphasis here. Once a premium square has been covered by a tile, it has no effect on any subsequent moves, even though the word covering that square may be modified on a later move.)

The total score for the move is the sum of the scores of the individual words.

So, how do you work out the score for the individual words?

When a letter tile covers a grey square, its point value remains the same.

When a tile covers a light blue (2L) square, its point value is *doubled*. When it covers a dark blue (3L) square, its point value is *tripled*.

When a tile covers a pink (2W) square, the point value for the whole word is *doubled*. And when a tile covers a red (3W) square, the point value for the whole word is *tripled*.

The effects of the premium squares are cumulative. If a word covers a light blue (2L) square and a pink (2W) square, the effect of the 2L square is calculated before doubling the score for the whole word. Similarly, if a word covers a dark blue (3L) square and a pink (2W) square, the effect of the 3L square is calculated before tripling the score for the whole word.

If a word should cover two pink (2W) squares, then the score for the word is doubled *and doubled again* (quadrupling the word's score!). And if a word covers two red (3W) squares, then the score for the word is tripled *and tripled again* (multiplying the word's score by 9!). Scrabble players often refer to such words as 'four-timers' and 'nine-timers'.

The Blank Tiles

You have already seen that two of the 100 tiles in a set are blank tiles. These bear no letters or point values. They can be used to represent any letter that a player wishes. When a blank tile is played, the player should declare what letter it is representing. Once the blank has been played, its letter value cannot be changed during the remainder of the game. The same applies to the other blank. Of course, it can be used to represent a different letter to the first blank, but once placed on the board, it retains its letter value until the end of the game.

Although the blanks have no point value, they are the two most valuable tiles in a set. This is because they enable you to squeeze additional points from the tiles that they are played in conjunction with, especially the high-value tiles (J, Q, X and Z), and because of their usefulness in helping to get 50-point bonuses. What is a 50-point bonus, you may be wondering. Well . . .

50-point Bonuses

A player is awarded a 50-point bonus if he uses all seven of the tiles on his rack at one turn. The word (or words) played have their score calculated in the standard way, taking into account the effects of premium squares, and then the 50-point bonus is added. The 50-point bonus is *not* added before any doubling and tripling is carried out. Of course, if you can manage to use all seven tiles on more than one occasion in a game, your score will receive a healthy boost! Later sections of the book will explain how to work towards getting these bonuses, rather than just hoping they will happen.

Scoring Examples

Perhaps a clutch of examples illustrating these various points would be helpful. In each of the examples that follows, an initial board position and a final board position are shown, so that it is quite clear what letters are being played on a particular move. In general, the initial board position of each example follows on from the final board position of the previous example. However, there are some exceptions, where it has been necessary to insert additional words in order to demonstrate a particular aspect of scoring. In some of the diagrams, in order to save space, an incomplete board is shown. Missing rows or columns are represented by a single shaded row or column. This shading convention will be used elsewhere, to signify missing rows and columns.

Figure 16 shows the first move in a game. The word FLEX has been played, starting at square E8 and going across. Since it covers the pink (2W) square at the centre of the board, the sum of the letter point values must be doubled. The score for FLEX – and for the move, since no other words are involved – is:

$$F + L + E + X \qquad = (4 + 1 + 1 + 8) \times 2$$
$$= 28 \text{ points}$$

Figure 17 shows the word NEXT being played, by adding N, E and T around the X already on the board. No premium squares have been covered on this move. Although there is a 2W square under the X, it was covered on the previous move, so has no effect on the scoring for this move. The score for NEXT, and the move, is:

$$N + E + X + T \qquad = 1 + 1 + 8 + 1$$
$$= 11 \text{ points}$$

Figure 18 shows the word REFLEX being played, using FLEX which is already on the board. A 2L square has been covered on this move by the first E of REFLEX. Again, the 2W square beneath the X plays no part in the scoring for this move, having been covered earlier. The score for REFLEX, and the move, is:

$$R + E + F + L + E + X \qquad = 1 + (1 \times 2) + 4 + 1 + 1 + 8$$
$$= 17 \text{ points}$$

Figure 19 shows the word ZOO being played on the board. Since the second O is above the R of REFLEX, the vertical word OR has also been formed. The score for the move will be the sum of the scores for the words ZOO and OR individually. Note that the 2L square under the O contributes to the scores of both ZOO and OR. So, the scores for the individual words are:

Z + O + O	= 10 + 1 + (1 × 2)
	= 13 points
O + R	= (1 × 2) + 1
	= 3 points

Hence the score for the move is 13 + 3, or 16, points.

Figure 20 shows the word AREA being played parallel to NEXT. Four words have been made (AREA, AN, RE and AT), and the total score for the move will be the sum of their individual scores. Note that both the R and second A of AREA cover 2L squares. The scores for the individual words are:

A + R + E + A	= 1 + (1 × 2) + 1 + (1 × 2)
	= 6 points
A + N	= 1 + 1
	= 2 points
R + E	= (1 × 2) + 1
	= 3 points
A + T	= (1 × 2) + 1
	= 3 points

Hence, the score for the move is 6 + 2 + 3 + 3, or 14, points.

Figure 21 shows the word UNDO being played, with the D covering a dark blue (3L) square. The score for the word, and the move, is:

U + N + D + O	= 1 + 1 + (2 × 3) + 1
	= 9 points

Figure 22 shows the word HEAP being played vertically. The P also turns the existing word AN into PAN. The P covers a dark blue (3L) square, so the P in HEAP will be tripled, as well as the P in PAN. The scores for the individual words are:

H + E + A + P	= 4 + 1 + 1 + (3 × 3)
	= 15 points
P + A + N	= (3 × 3) + 1 + 1
	= 11 points

The score for the move is $15 + 11$, or 26, points. This example shows how scores can start to mount up when playing two words (one vertically, and one horizontally) with a high- or medium-value letter on a premium letter score square (especially a 3L one).

Figure 23 shows the word CROOK being placed on the board, with the C and K both being on 3L squares. The vertical word HEAP is modified to CHEAP at the same time. The scores are:

$$C+R+O+O+K \quad = (3 \times 3)+1+1+1+(5 \times 3)$$
$$= 27 \text{ points}$$

$$C+H+E+A+P \quad = (3 \times 3)+4+1+1+3$$
$$= 18 \text{ points}$$

The whole move scores a total of 45 points. Again, the value of making two words with an intersecting high- or medium-value letter on a premium letter score square is amply demonstrated.

Figure 24 shows the word MYTH being played, and covering a pink (2W) square. This scores:

$$M+Y+T+H \quad = (3+4+1+4) \times 2$$
$$= 24 \text{ points}$$

Notice how the point values of all the letters are added up (12 points) before applying the effect of the 2W square, ie doubling the 12 points. Using a medium- or high-value letter, like the H here, to form part of a premium word score square can help build up your points quite effectively.

Figure 25 shows the letters H and E being played parallel to the EA in CHEAP, making the words THE, HE and EA. (Don't worry if you don't recognize the word EA yet. It will become more familiar once the two-letter words are examined in detail.) Both THE and EA cover the same 2W square on this move. The individual word scores are:

$$T+H+E \quad = (1+4+1) \times 2$$
$$= 12 \text{ points}$$

$$H+E \quad = 4+1$$
$$= 5 \text{ points}$$

$$E+A \quad = (1+1) \times 2$$
$$= 4 \text{ points}$$

Adding these word scores together gives a total of 21 points for the move.

Figure 26 shows the letters I and P being added beneath the Z of ZOO. As ZIP covers a red (3W) square on this move. The score for the word, and the move, is:

Z + I + P $= (10 + 1 + 3) \times 3$
                        $= 42$ points

This example hints at the power of the 3W squares, especially when covered by a word containing a high-value letter.

Figure 27 sees the word OWT played parallel to the ROO of CROOK. (If you don't know OWT, it's a dialect word for 'anything', as in the phrase 'you don't get owt for nowt'.) The 3W square has just been covered by two words: OWT and WO. So the point values for both these words will need to be tripled. Additionally, two other vertical words have been made, OR and TO. The scores are:

O + W + T $= (1 + 4 + 1) \times 3$
                        $= 18$ points

O + R $= 1 + 1$
                        $= 2$ points

W + O $= (4 + 1) \times 3$
                        $= 15$ points

T + O $= 1 + 1$
                        $= 2$ points

This gives a total of 37 points for the move.

Figure 28 shows the letters W, A and S being played around the Y of MYTH, making the two words WAYS and SHE. Note that the W covers a 2L square, and the S (in both WAYS and SHE) covers a 2W square. The word scores here are:

W + A + Y + S $= ((4 \times 2) + 1 + 4 + 1) \times 2$
                        $= 28$ points

S + H + E $= (1 + 4 + 1) \times 2$
                        $= 12$ points

And the score for the move is 40 points.

Figure 29 shows the word QUAY being played downwards

from square A1. The two-letter word YU is also made at the same time. (Again, if you don't know YU, you will become familiar with it later on.) The Y covers a 2L square, which occurs in both the words played, and QUAY covers a 3W square. The word scores are:

$$Q + U + A + Y \qquad = (10 + 1 + 1 + (4 \times 2)) \times 3$$
$$= 60 \text{ points}$$

$$Y + U \qquad = (4 \times 2) + 1$$
$$= 9 \text{ points}$$

The total score for the move is a very respectable 69 points! These sorts of scores can often be obtained by slotting in words using the high-value letters covering one of the 3W squares.

Figure 30 shows the word OVERDO covering both a 3L and a 2W square, also making another of those two-letter words, PO, in the process. The word scores here are:

$$O + V + E + R + D + O \qquad = (1 + (4 \times 3) + 1 + 1 + 2 + 1) \times 2$$
$$= 36 \text{ points}$$

$$P + O \qquad = 3 + 1$$
$$= 4 \text{ points}$$

And the move score is 40 points.

The initial board position in Figure 31 is not the same as the final board position in Figure 30. The word PAN has been extended to PANELLED. In Figure 31, the word FLAMING is played through the second L of PANELLED, covering two 2W squares, effectively quadrupling the point values of the letters in FLAMING. The score for FLAMING, and the whole move, is:

$$F + L + A + M + I + N + G \qquad = ((4 + 1 + 1 + 3 + 1 + 1 + 2) \times 2) \times 2$$
$$= 52 \text{ points}$$

The initial board position in Figure 32 is not the same as the final board position in Figure 31. The words GIBLET and TAR have been added. In Figure 32, the letters S, V, I, N and G are played around TAR, already on the board, to make the eight-letter word STARVING. Since STARVING covers two 3W squares, the point value for the word will need to be tripled and tripled again. Don't overlook the fact that the V is on a 2L square also. Thus:

$$S+T+A+R+V+I+N+G = ((1+1+1+1+(4 \times 2)$$
$$+1+1+2) \times 3) \times 3$$
$$= 144 \text{ points!}$$

Notice how the V alone has contributed half of these points. The 4-point V is on a 2L square (giving 8 points), and this has been tripled and tripled again, hence 72 points for the V itself. Needless to say, moves like this are few and far between, but by no means unknown!

Figure 33 shows the word VIRUS being played, using a V already on the board and using a blank tile as an S. (The blank-as-an-S is shown as S* in the diagram.) The blank tile covers a premium letter square – a 3L square in this case. The effect of this 3L square is to triple the value of the blank, and since zero tripled is still zero, there is no real scoring contribution from the blank. It has merely enabled its player to put down the other three tiles – IRU. The score for the move is:

$$V+I+R+U+S^* \qquad = 4+1+1+1+(0 \times 3)$$
$$= 7 \text{ points}$$

Figure 34 shows the word BRAID being played, using an R already on the board and using the second blank tile as an I. (The blank-as-an-I is shown as I* in the diagram.) The word BRAID covers a premium word square – a 2W square in this case. It doesn't matter that the actual tile on the 2W square is a blank – as long as the word covers the 2W square, then its points will be doubled. The score for the move is:

$$B+R+A+I^*+D \qquad = ((3 \times 2)+1+1+0+2) \times 2$$
$$= 20 \text{ points}$$

Figure 35 shows the word JUNCTION being played. Seven tiles have been added to an existing N, thereby qualifying its player for a 50-point bonus, in addition to whatever JUNCTION itself scores. Note that the first N covers a 3L square, and the whole word covers a 2W square. The total score for the move is:

$$J+U+N+C+T+I+O+N = (8+1+(1 \times 3)+3+1$$
$$+1+1+1) \times 2+50$$
$$= 88 \text{ points}$$

	A	B	C	D	E	F	G	H	I	J	K	L	M	N	O
1	3W			2L				3W				2L			3W
2		2W				3L				3L				2W	
3			2W				2L		2L				2W		
4	2L			2W				2L				2W			2L
5					2W						2W				
6		3L				3L				3L				3L	
7			2L				2L		2L				2L		
8	3W			2L	F	L	E	X				2L			3W
9			2L				2L		2L				2L		
10		3L				3L				3L				3L	

Figure 16: First move, covering the central 2W premium square

	A	B	C	D	E	F	G	H	I	J	K	L	M	N	O
1	3W			2L				3W				2L			3W
2		2W				3L				3L				2W	
3			2W				2L		2L				2W		
4	2L			2W				2L				2W			2L
5					2W						2W				
6		3L				3L	N			3L				3L	
7			2L				2L	E	2L				2L		
8	3W			2L	F	L	E	X				2L			3W
9			2L				2L	T	2L				2L		
10		3L				3L				3L				3L	

Figure 17: No premium squares covered

	A	B	C	D	E	F	G	H	I	J	K	L	M	N	O
1	3W			2L				3W				2L			3W
2		2W				3L				3L				2W	
3			2W				2L		2L				2W		
4	2L			2W				2L				2W			2L
5					2W						2W				
6		3L				3L		N		3L				3L	
7			2L				2L	E	2L				2L		
8	3W			2L	F	L	E	X				2L			3W
9			2L				2L	T	2L				2L		
10		3L				3L				3L				3L	

	A	B	C	D	E	F	G	H	I	J	K	L	M	N	O
1	3W			2L				3W				2L			3W
2		2W				3L				3L				2W	
3			2W				2L		2L				2W		
4	2L			2W				2L				2W			2L
5					2W						2W				
6		3L				3L		N		3L				3L	
7			2L				2L	E	2L				2L		
8	3W		R	E	F	L	E	X				2L			3W
9			2L				2L	T	2L				2L		
10		3L				3L				3L				3L	

Figure 18: A 2L square covered

First grid (A–O columns, rows 1–10) with premium squares and the word REFLEX placed across row 8 (C8–H8) and NEXT placed vertically in column H (H6–H9):

	A	B	C	D	E	F	G	H	I	J	K	L	M	N	O
1	3W			2L				3W				2L			3W
2		2W				3L				3L				2W	
3			2W				2L		2L				2W		
4	2L			2W				2L				2W			2L
5					2W						2W				
6		3L				3L		N		3L				3L	
7			2L				2L	E	2L				2L		
8	3W		R	E	F	L	E	X				2L			3W
9			2L				2L	T	2L				2L		
10		3L				3L				3L				3L	

Second grid with ZOO added in row 7 (A7–C7):

	A	B	C	D	E	F	G	H	I	J	K	L	M	N	O
1	3W			2L				3W				2L			3W
2		2W				3L				3L				2W	
3			2W				2L		2L				2W		
4	2L			2W				2L				2W			2L
5					2W						2W				
6		3L				3L		N		3L				3L	
7	Z	O	O				2L	E	2L				2L		
8	3W		R	E	F	L	E	X				2L			3W
9			2L				2L	T	2L				2L		
10		3L				3L				3L				3L	

Figure 19: A 2L square covered by two words

	A	B	C	D	E	F	G	H	I	J	K	L	M	N	O
1	3W			2L				3W				2L			3W
2		2W				3L				3L				2W	
3			2W				2L		2L				2W		
4	2L			2W				2L				2W			2L
5					2W						2W				
6		3L				3L		N		3L				3L	
7	Z	O	O				2L	E	2L				2L		
8	3W		R	E	F	L	E	X				2L			3W
9			2L				2L	T	2L				2L		
10		3L				3L				3L				3L	

	A	B	C	D	E	F	G	H	I	J	K	L	M	N	O
1	3W			2L				3W				2L			3W
2		2W				3L				3L				2W	
3			2W				2L		2L				2W		
4	2L			2W				2L				2W			2L
5					2W						2W				
6		3L				3L	A	N		3L				3L	
7	Z	O	O				R	E	2L				2L		
8	3W		R	E	F	L	E	X				2L			3W
9			2L				A	T	2L				2L		
10		3L				3L				3L				3L	

Figure 20: Two 2L squares covered

	A	B	C	D	E	F	G	H	I	J	K	L	M	N	O
1	3W			2L				3W				2L			3W
2		2W				3L				3L				2W	
3			2W				2L		2L				2W		
4	2L			2W				2L				2W			2L
5					2W						2W				
6		3L				3L	A	N		3L				3L	
7	Z	O	O				R	E	2L				2L		
8	3W		R	E	F	L	E	X				2L			3W
9		2L					A	T	2L				2L		
10		3L				3L				3L				3L	

	A	B	C	D	E	F	G	H	I	J	K	L	M	N	O
1	3W			2L				3W				2L			3W
2		2W				3L				3L				2W	
3			2W				2L		2L				2W		
4	2L	U		2W				2L				2W			2L
5		N			2W						2W				
6		D				3L	A	N		3L				3L	
7	Z	O	O				R	E	2L				2L		
8	3W		R	E	F	L	E	X				2L			3W
9		2L					A	T	2L				2L		
10		3L				3L				3L				3L	

Figure 21: A 3L square covered

	A	B	C	D	E	F	G	H	I	J	K	L	M	N	O
1	3W			2L			3W					2L			3W
2		2W				3L				3L				2W	
3			2W				2L		2L				2W		
4	2L	U		2W				2L				2W			2L
5		N			2W						2W				
6		D				3L	A	N		3L				3L	
7	Z	O	O				R	E	2L				2L		
8	3W		R	E	F	L	E	X				2L			3W
9			2L				A	T	2L				2L		
10		3L				3L				3L				3L	

	A	B	C	D	E	F	G	H	I	J	K	L	M	N	O
1	3W			2L			3W					2L			3W
2		2W				3L				3L				2W	
3			2W			H	2L		2L				2W		
4	2L	U		2W		E		2L				2W			2L
5		N			2W	A					2W				
6		D				P	A	N		3L				3L	
7	Z	O	O				R	E	2L				2L		
8	3W		R	E	F	L	E	X				2L			3W
9			2L				A	T	2L				2L		
10		3L				3L				3L				3L	

Figure 22: A 3L square covered using two words

Top board:

	A	B	C	D	E	F	G	H	I	J	K	L	M	N	O
1	3W			2L				3W				2L			3W
2		2W				3L				3L				2W	
3			2W			H	2L		2L				2W		
4	2L	U		2W		E		2L				2W			2L
5		N			2W	A					2W				
6		D				P	A	N		3L				3L	
7	Z	O	O				R	E	2L				2L		
8	3W		R	E	F	L	E	X				2L			3W
9			2L				A	T	2L				2L		
10		3L				3L				3L				3L	

Bottom board:

	A	B	C	D	E	F	G	H	I	J	K	L	M	N	O
1	3W			2L				3W				2L			3W
2		2W				C	R	O	O	K				2W	
3			2W			H	2L		2L				2W		
4	2L	U		2W		E		2L				2W			2L
5		N			2W	A					2W				
6		D				P	A	N		3L				3L	
7	Z	O	O				R	E	2L				2L		
8	3W		R	E	F	L	E	X				2L			3W
9			2L				A	T	2L				2L		
10		3L				3L				3L				3L	

Figure 23: Two 3L squares covered

	A	B	C	D	E	F	G	H	I	J	K	L	M	N	O
1	3W			2L				3W				2L			3W
2		2W				C	R	O	O	K				2W	
3			2W			H	2L		2L				2W		
4	2L	U		2W		E		2L			2W				2L
5		N			2W	A				2W					
6		D				P	A	N		3L				3L	
7	Z	O	O				R	E	2L				2L		
8	3W		R	E	F	L	E	X				2L			3W
9			2L				A	T	2L				2L		
10		3L				3L				3L				3L	

	A	B	C	D	E	F	G	H	I	J	K	L	M	N	O
1	3W			2L				3W				2L			3W
2		2W				C	R	O	O	K				2W	
3			M	Y	T	H	2L		2L				2W		
4	2L	U		2W		E		2L			2W				2L
5		N			2W	A				2W					
6		D				P	A	N		3L				3L	
7	Z	O	O				R	E	2L				2L		
8	3W		R	E	F	L	E	X				2L			3W
9			2L				A	T	2L				2L		
10		3L				3L				3L				3L	

Figure 24: A 2W square covered

	A	B	C	D	E	F	G	H	I	J	K	L	M	N	O
1	3W			2L				3W				2L			3W
2		2W				C	R	O	O	K				2W	
3			M	Y	T	H	2L		2L				2W		
4	2L	U		2W		E		2L				2W			2L
5		N			2W	A					2W				
6		D				P	A	N		3L				3L	
7	Z	O	O				R	E	2L			2L			
8	3W		R	E	F	L	E	X				2L			3W
9			2L				A	T	2L			2L			
10		3L				3L				3L				3L	

	A	B	C	D	E	F	G	H	I	J	K	L	M	N	O
1	3W			2L				3W				2L			3W
2		2W				C	R	O	O	K				2W	
3			M	Y	T	H	2L		2L				2W		
4	2L	U		2W	H	E		2L				2W			2L
5		N			E	A					2W				
6		D				P	A	N		3L				3L	
7	Z	O	O				R	E	2L			2L			
8	3W		R	E	F	L	E	X				2L			3W
9			2L				A	T	2L			2L			
10		3L				3L				3L				3L	

Figure 25: A 2W square covered in two directions

	A	B	C	D	E	F	G	H	I	J	K	L	M	N	O
1	3W			2L				3W				2L			3W
2		2W				C	R	O	O	K				2W	
3			M	Y	T	H	2L		2L				2W		
4	2L	U		2W	H	E		2L				2W			2L
5		N			E	A					2W				
6		D				P	A	N		3L				3L	
7	Z	O	O				R	E	2L				2L		
8	3W		R	E	F	L	E	X				2L			3W
9			2L				A	T	2L				2L		
10		3L				3L				3L				3L	

	A	B	C	D	E	F	G	H	I	J	K	L	M	N	O
1	3W			2L				3W				2L			3W
2		2W				C	R	O	O	K				2W	
3			M	Y	T	H	2L		2L				2W		
4	2L	U		2W	H	E		2L				2W			2L
5		N			E	A					2W				
6		D				P	A	N		3L				3L	
7	Z	O	O				R	E	2L				2L		
8	I		R	E	F	L	E	X				2L			3W
9	P		2L				A	T	2L				2L		
10		3L				3L				3L				3L	

Figure 26: A 3W square covered

	A	B	C	D	E	F	G	H	I	J	K	L	M	N	O
1	3W			2L				3W				2L			3W
2		2W				C	R	O	O	K				2W	
3			M	Y	T	H	2L		2L				2W		
4	2L	U		2W	H	E		2L				2W			2L
5		N			E	A					2W				
6		D				P	A	N		3L			3L		
7	Z	O	O				R	E	2L			2L			
8	I		R	E	F	L	E	X				2L			3W
9	P		2L				A	T	2L			2L			
10		3L				3L			3L				3L		

	A	B	C	D	E	F	G	H	I	J	K	L	M	N	O
1	3W			2L			O	W	T			2L			3W
2		2W				C	R	O	O	K				2W	
3			M	Y	T	H	2L		2L				2W		
4	2L	U		2W	H	E		2L				2W			2L
5		N			E	A					2W				
6		D				P	A	N		3L			3L		
7	Z	O	O				R	E	2L			2L			
8	I		R	E	F	L	E	X				2L			3W
9	P		2L				A	T	2L			2L			
10		3L				3L			3L				3L		

Figure 27: A 3W square covered in two directions

	A	B	C	D	E	F	G	H	I	J	K	L	M	N	O
1	3W			2L			O	W	T			2L			3W
2		2W				C	R	O	O	K				2W	
3			M	Y	T	H	2L		2L				2W		
4	2L	U		2W	H	E		2L				2W			2L
5		N			E	A					2W				
6		D				P	A	N		3L				3L	
7	Z	O	O				R	E	2L				2L		
8	I		R	E	F	L	E	X				2L			3W
9	P		2L				A	T	2L				2L		
10		3L				3L			3L			3L			

	A	B	C	D	E	F	G	H	I	J	K	L	M	N	O
1	3W			W			O	W	T			2L			3W
2		2W		A		C	R	O	O	K				2W	
3			M	Y	T	H	2L		2L				2W		
4	2L	U		S	H	E		2L				2W			2L
5		N			E	A					2W				
6		D				P	A	N		3L				3L	
7	Z	O	O				R	E	2L				2L		
8	I		R	E	F	L	E	X				2L			3W
9	P		2L				A	T	2L				2L		
10		3L				3L			3L			3L			

Figure 28: 2L and 2W squares covered

	A	B	C	D	E	F	G	H	I	J	K	L	M	N	O
1	3W			W			O	W	T			2L			3W
2		2W		A		C	R	O	O	K				2W	
3			M	Y	T	H	2L		2L				2W		
4	2L	U		S	H	E		2L				2W			2L
5		N			E	A					2W				
6		D				P	A	N		3L				3L	
7	Z	O	O				R	E	2L				2L		
8	I		R	E	F	L	E	X				2L			3W
9	P		2L				A	T	2L				2L		
10		3L				3L				3L				3L	

	A	B	C	D	E	F	G	H	I	J	K	L	M	N	O
1	Q			W			O	W	T			2L			3W
2	U	2W		A		C	R	O	O	K				2W	
3	A		M	Y	T	H	2L		2L				2W		
4	Y	U		S	H	E		2L				2W			2L
5		N			E	A					2W				
6		D				P	A	N		3L				3L	
7	Z	O	O				R	E	2L				2L		
8	I		R	E	F	L	E	X				2L			3W
9	P		2L				A	T	2L				2L		
10		3L				3L				3L				3L	

Figure 29: 2L and 3W squares covered

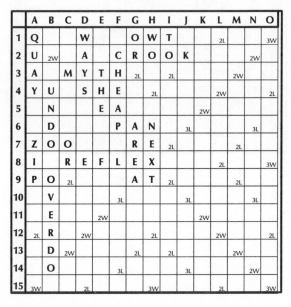

Figure 30: 3L and 2W squares covered

	A	B	C	D	E	F	G	H	I	J	K	L	M	N	O
1	Q			W			O	W	T			2L			3W
2	U	2W		A		C	R	O	O	K				2W	
3	A		M	Y	T	H	2L		2L				2W		
4	Y	U		S	H	E		2L				2W			2L
5		N			E	A					2W				
6		D				P	A	N	E	L	L	E	D	3L	
7	Z	O	O				R	E	2L				2L		
8	I		R	E	F	L	E	X				2L			3W
9	P	O	2L				A	T	2L				2L		
10		V				3L				3L				3L	
11		E			2W						2W				
12	2L	R		2W				2L				2W			2L
13		D	2W				2L		2L				2W		
14		O				3L				3L				2W	
15	3W			2L				3W				2L			3W

	A	B	C	D	E	F	G	H	I	J	K	L	M	N	O
1	Q			W			O	W	T			2L			3W
2	U	2W		A		C	R	O	O	K				2W	
3	A		M	Y	T	H	2L		2L				2W		
4	Y	U		S	H	E		2L				2W			2L
5		N			E	A					F				
6		D				P	A	N	E	L	L	E	D	3L	
7	Z	O	O				R	E	2L		A		2L		
8	I		R	E	F	L	E	X			M	2L			3W
9	P	O	2L				A	T	2L		I		2L		
10		V				3L				3L	N			3L	
11		E			2W						G				
12	2L	R		2W				2L				2W			2L
13		D	2W				2L		2L				2W		
14		O				3L				3L				2W	
15	3W			2L				3W				2L			3W

Figure 31: Two 2W squares covered

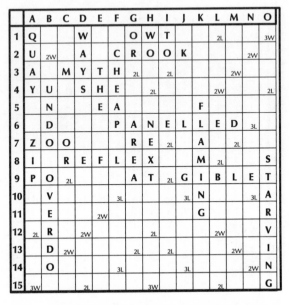

	A	B	C	D	E	F	G	H	I	J	K	L	M	N	O
1	Q			W			O	W	T			2L			3W
2	U	2W		A		C	R	O	O	K				2W	
3	A		M	Y	T	H	2L		2L				2W		
4	Y	U		S	H	E		2L				2W			2L
5		N			E	A					F				
6		D				P	A	N	E	L	L	E	D	3L	
7	Z	O	O				R	E	2L		A		2L		
8	I		R	E	F	L	E	X			M	2L			3W
9	P	O	2L				A	T	2L	G	I	B	L	E	T
10		V			3L					3L	N			3L	A
11		E		2W							G				R
12	2L	R		2W				2L					2W		2L
13		D	2W				2L		2L					2W	
14		O			3L					3L				2W	
15	3W			2L			3W					2L			3W

	A	B	C	D	E	F	G	H	I	J	K	L	M	N	O
1	Q			W			O	W	T			2L			3W
2	U	2W		A		C	R	O	O	K				2W	
3	A		M	Y	T	H	2L		2L				2W		
4	Y	U		S	H	E		2L				2W			2L
5		N			E	A					F				
6		D				P	A	N	E	L	L	E	D	3L	
7	Z	O	O				R	E	2L		A		2L		
8	I		R	E	F	L	E	X			M	2L			S
9	P	O	2L				A	T	2L	G	I	B	L	E	T
10		V			3L					3L	N			3L	A
11		E		2W							G				R
12	2L	R		2W				2L					2W		V
13		D	2W				2L		2L					2W	I
14		O			3L					3L				2W	N
15	3W			2L			3W					2L			G

Figure 32: Two 3W squares covered

	A	B	C	D	E	F	G	H	I	J	K	L	M	N	O
1	Q			W			O	W	T			2L			3W
2	U	2W		A		C	R	O	O	K				2W	
3	A		M	Y	T	H	2L		2L				2W		
4	Y	U		S	H	E		2L				2W			2L
5		N			E	A					F				
6		D				P	A	N	E	L	L	E	D	3L	
7	Z	O	O				R	E	2L		A		2L		
8	I		R	E	F	L	E	X			M	2L			S
9	P	O	2L				A	T	2L	G	I	B	L	E	T
10		V			3L					3L	N			3L	A
11		E		2W							G				R
12	2L	R	2W				2L					2W			V
13		D	2W				2L		2L				2W		I
14		O			3L					3L				2W	N
15	3W			2L			3W					2L			G

	A	B	C	D	E	F	G	H	I	J	K	L	M	N	O
1	Q			W			O	W	T			2L			3W
2	U	2W		A		C	R	O	O	K				2W	
3	A		M	Y	T	H	2L		2L				2W		
4	Y	U		S	H	E		2L				2W			2L
5		N			E	A					F				
6		D				P	A	N	E	L	L	E	D	3L	
7	Z	O	O				R	E	2L		A		2L		
8	I		R	E	F	L	E	X			M	2L			S
9	P	O	2L				A	T	2L	G	I	B	L	E	T
10		V	I	R	U	S*				3L	N			3L	A
11		E			2W						G				R
12	2L	R		2W				2L				2W			V
13		D	2W				2L		2L				2W		I
14		O			3L					3L				2W	N
15	3W			2L			3W					2L			G

Figure 33: A blank on a premium letter square

	A	B	C	D	E	F	G	H	I	J	K	L	M	N	O
1	Q			W			O	W	T			2L			3W
2	U	2W		A		C	R	O	O	K				2W	
3	A		M	Y	T	H	2L		2L				2W		
4	Y	U		S	H	E		2L				2W			2L
5		N			E	A					F				
6		D				P	A	N	E	L	L	E	D	3L	
7	Z	O	O				R	E	2L		A		2L		
8	I		R	E	F	L	E	X			M	2L			S
9	P	O	2L				A	T	2L	G	I	B	L	E	T
10		V	I	R	U	S*				3L	N			3L	A
11		E			2W						G				R
12	2L	R		2W				2L				2W			V
13		D	2W				2L		2L				2W		I
14		O				3L					3L			2W	N
15	3W			2L				3W					2L		G

	A	B	C	D	E	F	G	H	I	J	K	L	M	N	O
1	Q			W			O	W	T			2L			3W
2	U	2W		A		C	R	O	O	K				2W	
3	A		M	Y	T	H	2L		2L				2W		
4	Y	U		S	H	E		2L				2W			2L
5		N			E	A					F				
6		D				P	A	N	E	L	L	E	D	3L	
7	Z	O	O				R	E	2L		A		2L		
8	I		R	E	F	L	E	X			M	2L			S
9	P	O	2L				A	T	2L	G	I	B	L	E	T
10		V	I	R	U	S*				3L	N			3L	A
11		E			2W						G				R
12	B	R	A	I*	D			2L				2W			V
13		D	2W				2L		2L				2W		I
14		O				3L					3L			2W	N
15	3W			2L				3W					2L		G

Figure 34: A blank on a premium word square

	A	B	C	D	E	F	G	H	I	J	K	L	M	N	O
1	Q			W			O	W	T			2L			3W
2	U	2W		A		C	R	O	O	K				2W	
3	A		M	Y	T	H	2L		2L			2W			
4	Y	U		S	H	E		2L			2W				2L
5		N			E	A				F					
6		D				P	A	N	E	L	L	E	D	3L	
7	Z	O	O				R	E	2L		A		2L		
8	I		R	E	F	L	E	X			M	2L			S
9	P	O	2L				A	T	2L	G	I	B	L	E	T
10		V	I	R	U	S*			3L	N			3L	A
11		E			2W						G				R
12	B	R	A	I*	D			2L				2W			V
13		D	2W				2L		2L				2W		I
14		O				3L				3L				2W	N
15	3W			2L				3W				2L			G

	A	B	C	D	E	F	G	H	I	J	K	L	M	N	O
1	Q			W			O	W	T			2L			3W
2	U	2W		A		C	R	O	O	K				2W	
3	A		M	Y	T	H	2L		2L			2W			
4	Y	U		S	H	E		2L			2W				2L
5		N			E	A				F					
6		D				P	A	N	E	L	L	E	D	3L	
7	Z	O	O				R	E	2L		A		2L		
8	I		R	E	F	L	E	X			M	2L			S
9	P	O	2L				A	T	2L	G	I	B	L	E	T
10		V	I	R	U	S*			3L	N			3L	A
11		E			2W						G				R
12	B	R	A	I*	D			2L				2W			V
13		D	2W				2L		2L				2W		I
14		O				3L	J	U	N	C	T	I	O	N	N
15	3W			2L				3W				2L			G

Figure 35: A 50-point bonus

By now, you should be able to calculate the score for a move of any complexity – that is, any combination of 2L, 3L, 2W and 3W squares, blank tiles, and with or without a 50-point bonus. Figures 36-38 show three complex moves, involving various words and premium squares. See if you can work out the scores of the three moves involved – involving the block-busting words ARTICHOKES, RESONATE and EARTHMOVERS. (Answers are given in Chapter 10.)

	A	B	C	D	E	F	G	H	I	J	K	L	M	N	O
1	3W			2L			3W					2L			3W
2		2W				3L				3L				2W	
3			E				2L		2L				2W		
4	2L		Q	2W				T				T			2L
5			U		2W		G	R	A	M	M	A	R	S	
6		3L	I			3L		E		A		N		O	D
7			P	U	F	F	2L	A	2L	R		G	2L		O
8	3W			2L		A	R	T				2L			3W
9			2L			B	E	E	2L	H	I		I	R	E
10		3L				L		D		3L	T	O	N	E	
11					Z	E	L				C				
12	2L			2W			A	L	I	G	H	T			2L
13		2W					X		2L				2W		
14		2W				3L				3L				2W	
15	3W			2L			3W					2L			3W

	A	B	C	D	E	F	G	H	I	J	K	L	M	N	O
1	3W			2L			3W					2L			3W
2		2W				3L				3L				2W	
3			E				2L		2L				2W		
4	2L		Q	2W				T				T			2L
5			U		2W		G	R	A	M	M	A	R	S	
6		3L	I			3L		E		A		N		O	D
7			P	U	F	F	2L	A	2L	R		G	2L		O
8	3W			2L		A	R	T	I	C	H*	O	K	E	S
9			2L			B	E	E	2L	H	I		I	R	E
10		3L				L		D		3L	T	O	N	E	
11					Z	E	L				C				
12	2L			2W			A	L	I	G	H	T			2L
13		2W					X		2L				2W		
14		2W				3L				3L				2W	
15	3W			2L			3W					2L			3W

Figure 36: What's the score for ARTICHOKES?

	A	B	C	D	E	F	G	H	I	J	K	L	M	N	O
1	3W			2L				3W				2L			3W
2		2W				3L		D	3L	W			2W		
3			2W				2L	U				O	2W		
4	2L			2W			2L	F	L	O	W				2L
5					2W			F	A	H					
6		3L				3L		Z	O	O			3L		
7			2L				B	O	X	Y			2L		
8	3W			Q	U	E	E	N				2L			3W
9			2L			Y	2L		2L				2L		
10		3L	C		R	E		H	3L				3L		
11	M		A		E			P	E	R	2W				
12	A	P	T	2W	A		S	2L	A	I	D	2W			2L
13	T	A	E	L	S		K	A	R	T	I	N	G		
14	E	R	R		O	M	I	T	T	E	D			2W	
15	3W			2L	N			3W				2L			3W

	A	B	C	D	E	F	G	H	I	J	K	L	M	N	O
1	3W			2L				3W				2L			3W
2		2W				3L		D	3L	W			2W		
3			2W				2L	U				O	2W		
4	2L			2W			2L	F	L	O	W				2L
5					2W			F	A	H					
6		3L				3L		Z	O	O			3L		
7			2L				B	O	X	Y			2L		
8	3W			Q	U	E	E	N				2L			3W
9			2L			Y	2L		2L				2L		
10		3L	C		R	E		H	3L				3L		
11	M		A		E			P	E	R	2W				
12	A	P	T	2W	A		S	2L	A	I	D	2W			2L
13	T	A	E	L	S		K	A	R	T	I	N	G		
14	E	R	R		O	M	I	T	T	E	D			2W	
15	R	E*	S	O	N	A	T	E				2L			3W

Figure 37: What's the score for RESONATE?

	A	B	C	D	E	F	G	H	I	J	K	L	M	N	O
1	3W			2L				3W				2L			3W
2		2W				W			3L				2W		
3			2W			H	2L		2L			2W			
4	2L			2W	L	A	T	E			J	2W			2L
5				A	I	M		X			O				
6		3L		R		3L	L	U	C	K	Y		3L		
7			2L	T				I	D	2L			2L		
8	3W			2L	O	B	O	E	S			2L			3W
9			2L	M		A	N		T				2L		
10		3L	D	O	Z	Y			A	3L			3L		
11					2W			P	R	I	G				
12	2L			2W	L	I	C	I	T			2W			2L
13			2W		E		2L	Q	2L				2W		
14		2W		S	E	W		U		3L				2W	
15	3W			2L				E				2L			3W

	A	B	C	D	E	F	G	H	I	J	K	L	M	N	O
1	3W			2L				3W				2L			3W
2		2W				W			3L				2W		
3			2W			H	2L		2L			2W			
4	2L			E	L	A	T	E			J	2W			2L
5				A	I	M		X			O				
6		3L		R		3L	L	U	C	K	Y		3L		
7			2L	T				I	D	2L			2L		
8	3W			H	O	B	O	E	S			2L			3W
9			2L	M		A	N		T				2L		
10		3L	D	O	Z	Y			A	3L			3L		
11				V	2W			P	R	I	G				
12	2L			E	L	I	C	I	T			2W			2L
13			2W	R	E		2L	Q	2L				2W		
14		2W		S	E	W		U		3L				2W	
15	3W			2L				E				2L			3W

Figure 38: What's the score for EARTHMOVERS?

Exchanging Tiles

When it's your turn, you can opt not to play a word, but to exchange some or all of your tiles for replacement ones from the bag of unchosen tiles. Why would you do this?

The tiles that you have may not make any words, even allowing for combination with letters already on the board. It quite often happens that you find yourself holding seven awkward consonants – perhaps, BCFGMVW – or seven vowels – maybe AAAIIIU. Even if you can make one or two words, you may decide that you don't relish being left with most of the same tiles on your next turn. In which case, you can exchange tiles.

Another reason for exchanging tiles is when you are reasonably confident about being able to get a 50-point bonus. Suppose you have six promising letters (such as AEINST) and one awkward one (a Y, maybe). You could choose to exchange just the Y, in the expectation that almost any other letter will combine with AEINST to make a seven-letter word, which you might be able to play on your next turn.

Later sections of the book will go into more detail about when and why to exchange tiles, which ones to exchange, and which to retain. For the time being, you only need to understand that exchanging is allowed and the mechanics of the process.

If a player decides to exchange tiles, he decides first of all which ones he wants to get rid of, he places them face down near the board, selects an equal number of replacement tiles from the bag, returns the unwanted tiles to the bag, and gives the bag a good shuffle. Play now passes to the next player.

Although the official Scrabble rules allow for exchanges at any stage during a game, regardless of how many or how few tiles are left in the bag, it is very common to find that players do not allow exchanges if there are fewer then seven tiles in the bag. This seven-tile minimum applies throughout Scrabble clubs and competitive Scrabble matches.

When the seven-tile minimum is in force, assuming there are seven or more tiles still in the bag, then a player will always be able to exchange up to all seven of his tiles. If there are fewer than seven tiles left, he will not be able to exchange at all.

If the seven-tile minimum is not in force, then, close to the end of a game, a player may find there are fewer tiles in the pool than he wishes to exchange. In which case, hard luck! He will only be able to exchange as many tiles as he will be able to take from the bag as replacements. He might want to change four tiles, but if there are only three left in the bag, he will only be allowed to put up to three tiles back.

There is usually no limit on the number of times that a player may exchange tiles during a game. Of course, if you change too often, you will find that your opponent is running away with the game, while you are busy putting tiles back and selecting new ones!

Passing Your Turn

A player may decide not to play a word or exchange tiles, but to just sit tight. In which case, the player merely announces that he is passing, and play moves to the next player. Why would anyone do this, missing a scoring opportunity and not wanting to select some replacement tiles? The usual reason is in the hope that the opponent will play a word containing a letter which will combine with the seven letters of the passing player on his next turn. For example, a player may be holding the seven letters ADEILNT. By themselves, they do not make a seven-letter word. But in combination with various other letters, especially vowels, they can be used to make an eight-letter word, thereby scoring a valuable 50-point bonus. The letters ADEILNT can combine with all of the following to make an eight-letter word:

A	(giving DENTALIA)
B	(giving BIDENTAL)
E	(giving ENTAILED)
F	(giving INFLATED)
G	(giving DELATING)
O	(giving DELATION)
P	(giving PANTILED)
U	(giving UNTAILED)
V	(giving DIVALENT)

Don't worry if you don't recognize most of these words! By the end of the book, though, you will be aware that these are the sorts of words which accomplished Scrabble players put down with alarming regularity!

These nine letters account for 44 of the tiles in a set, although two of them (AE) are already on the ADEILNT rack. There is quite a good chance that the opponent will play a word containing one of these, especially an A, E or O. When the necessary letter is played by the opponent, the passing player will triumphantly put down his eight-letter word, gaining a 50-point bonus for using all of his tiles in one go.

Of course, the problem with passing is that the opponent realizes that he is expected to put down a helpful letter, so makes sure that he puts down his word in some inaccessible part of the board. In which case, the passing player is still stuck!

Overall, passing your turn has little to recommend it. It is usually better to play a word or exchange some tiles.

Scoring at the End of a Game

A game normally comes to an end when a player has used up all his tiles and there are none left in the bag. He should announce the score for his final move, and then say 'And out!'. This signals to all the other players – perhaps one, perhaps three – that the player concerned has 'gone out' and the game is over. But scores still need to be adjusted to take account of the letters that the opponents have on their racks. Each opponent tots up the point values of the tiles on his rack, and his score is reduced by this number. Conversely, the player who has gone out has his total score increased by the sum of the point values of his opponent's remaining tiles.

In a four-player game, this can affect quite dramatically the score of the player who went out. After all, if each of the opponents is left with tiles totalling, say, 6 points, then the player who went out will have his total score increased by 18 points.

In a two-player game, the player who went out has his score increased by the point values of the tiles remaining on his single opponent's rack. This usually has less dramatic impact than in the four-player situation.

Figure 40 illustrates this adjustment of scores at the end of a four-player game. Beth was the player who went out, and just after her last turn the scores were:

Allan   133
Beth   142
Chas   168
Diane   141

Note that Chas was in the lead with a margin of 26 points. Allan was left with tiles worth 4 points on his rack (DET, perhaps), so his score reduced to 129; Chas was left with tiles worth 8 points on his rack (IIOOV, perhaps), so his score was reduced to 160; and Diane was left with tiles worth 10 points on her rack (the Q, maybe), so her score was reduced to 131 points. On the other hand, Beth's score was increased by Allan's 4 points, Chas's 8 points, and Diane's 10 points – a total of 22 points! So the final scores now look like this:

Allan   129
Beth   164
Chas   160
Diane   131

Beth now has a higher total number of points than any of the other three players.

The opening sentence of this section stated that a game normally comes to an end when one player has used up all his tiles and there are none left in the bag. There is an exception to this, though. Although all of the players may have tiles on their racks, perhaps none of them is able to make a move. This sometimes happens when all players are left with impossible-to-use letters. It is quite easy to imagine a two-player game where one player is stuck with a Q and the other is stuck with a V. There is nowhere for a Q or a V to be played on the board, so both players are unable to use up all of their letters. In this situation, both players' total scores are reduced by the point values of the tiles left on their individual racks – minus 4 for the player with the V, and minus 10 for the player with the Q. In this situation, no player has his score increased.

Challenges

Suppose your opponent plays a word which you don't know, or which you suspect may be spelled incorrectly. What happens? Once the 'word' has been played and the score announced, you are able to challenge it if you want to. Your

challenge must occur before the opponent takes his replacement tiles from the bag or before your turn proper – that is,
before you play any tiles, or decide to exchange tiles, or decide
to pass.

The official rules of the game say that any words found in a
standard dictionary are valid for Scrabble, except those
beginning with a capital letter, those which are foreign, and
those spelled with an apostrophe or a hyphen. Neither are
abbreviations allowed.

Once a word is challenged, it is looked up in an agreed
dictionary (agreed before the game starts!). If the word is
valid, it remains on the board, and the challenge fails. If the
word is invalid (not in the dictionary, spelled with an initial
capital letter, shown as foreign, spelled with an apostrophe or
hyphen, shown as an abbreviation, or just plain misspelled),
then the letter tiles just played are to be removed from the
board and returned to the rack of the offending player.
Effectively, that player loses his turn, and his score for that
turn is shown as zero points. The offending player does not get
a chance to play a replacement word! Once the challenge has
been resolved, the next player continues with his turn.

Note that there is no penalty for an incorrect challenge. You
can challenge each and every word that your opponents play.
The only problem is that the game will take a lot longer and
your opponents are likely to become exasperated!

Do note that a word can only be challenged immediately after
it has been played. A word cannot be challenged if another
turn has taken place, regardless of whether this involves
playing tiles, exchanging tiles, passing a turn, or even another
challenge (whether it is successful or not!). It is no good
challenging your opponent's non-existent 'word' YB half a
dozen turns later, exclaiming that you were looking at it
upside down, and thought it was BY!

Keeping Track of the Scores and Score-sheets
When you first buy a Scrabble set, there is a pad of score-
sheets included with the game. One of these standard score-
sheets is shown in Figure 39. It has eight columns, enabling
you to score a game with up to four players. The recommended

way of scoring is to record in each player's left-hand column his individual scores, with the running totals in the player's right-hand column. So, for each of the four possible players, there will be a move-by-move score and a running total. Even if a player doesn't make a score (because he chooses to exchange tiles, or pass his turn, or has his turn successfully challenged), you should record that on the score-sheet. In the examples which follow, these are indicated by 'exch', 'pass' and 'chall' on the score-sheets. Of course, you are free to use your own shortened forms, but you need to be able to distinguish between them. A dash may be insufficient, especially if there is a dispute afterwards over the scores, as you may be unable to reconstruct the precise moves and scores. One of the commonest errors in scoring is to omit an exchange of tiles or a challenged move, and then enter successive scores against the wrong player! By entering something on the score-sheet for every turn, you can ensure that you haven't missed any scores, exchanges, passes and challenges, as all players should be on the same number of turns, or perhaps one less because there hasn't been a complete round. Also, by recording the scores for individual turns, you can always go back and check the addition if there is any dispute about this later in the game.

Figure 40 shows a completed score-sheet for a game between four players – Allan, Beth, Chas and Diane.

If you usually play with only two players, a simplified score-sheet is shown in Figure 41. This has space for individual scores and running totals for just two players. This is perfectly adequate for most normal games of Scrabble.

However, some players may wish to record the letter tiles which they had on each turn, plus the words they and their opponent played, in addition to scores and running totals. An advanced score-sheet for doing this is shown in Figure 42. This score-sheet doesn't include a column for recording your opponent's letter tiles, as you won't have knowledge of these during the game.

Figure 43 shows a completed board after a game between Alice and Bobby. Figures 44 and 45 show completed score-sheets, based on the simple and advanced two-player score-sheets already described. You might find it helpful to reconstruct this game, checking the scoring for each move, to ensure that you agree with the scoring effects of the various combinations of premium squares, blank tiles, bonus moves, and non-scoring moves.

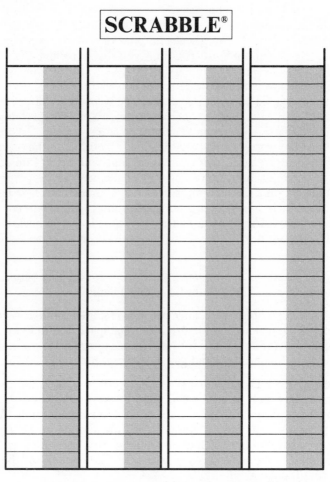

Figure 39: The standard Scrabble score-sheet

SCRABBLE®

Allan		Beth		Chas		Diane	
12	12	18	18	(exch)	0	20	20
6	18	20	38	66	66	15	35
16	34	7	45	24	90	21	56
19	53	2	47	14	104	25	81
11	64	48	95	12	116	26	107
32	96	17	112	26	142	5	112
8	104	(chall)	112	15	157	10	122
24	128	20	132	11	168	19	141
5	133	10	142				
−4	129	22	164	−8	160	−10	131

Figure 40: A completed standard Scrabble score-sheet

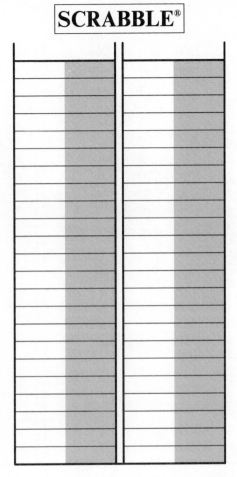

Figure 41: A 2-player score-sheet, based on the standard Scrabble
score-sheet

SCRABBLE®

My tiles	Words played	Score	Total	Words played	Score	Total

Figure 42: A 2-player score-sheet,
allowing tiles and words played to be recorded

	A	B	C	D	E	F	G	H	I	J	K	L	M	N	O
1	3W			2L				3W				A	V	O	W
2		T				3L				T	O		I	F	
3		R*	2W		E		2L		G	O			C		
4	2L	A		B	Y			J	U	N	G	L	E		2L
5		N		R	E			U	M		A				
6		S	K	I	D	3L		M		G	I			3L	
7		I	2L	E			2L	P	2L	I	N		2L		
8	A	T		F	I	L	L	Y			S	Q	U	A	W
9	U		2L			A	2L		2L				2L		O
10	T*	3L				Z				3L				3L	O
11	O			T	H	E					2W				D
12	S			R	E			2L		O	I	2W			S
13			R	E	P	L	A	N	T		C	R	A	B	
14		2W		E		3L		I		H	O	A	R	2W	
15	V	E	I	N			E	X	T	E	N	D	E	D	3W

Figure 43: A completed game,
the basis of the next two score-sheets

SCRABBLE®

Alice		Bobby	
30	30	20	20
23	53	33	53
(exch) 0	53	20	73
16	69	27	100
80	149	30	130
18	167	(exch) 0	130
30	197	69	199
28	225	35	234
31	256	(chall) 0	234
12	268	10	244
87	355	8	252
18	373	10	262
33	406	77	339
20	426	21	360
10	436	9	369
−5	431	5	374

Figure 44: A completed 2-player score-sheet,
containing scores and running totals

The Basics

SCRABBLE®

	Alice				*Bobby*		
My tiles	Words played	Score	Total		Words played	Score	Total
EFILLRY	FILLY	30	30		BRIEF	20	20
EEEQRVY	EYE, BY, RE	23	53		LAZE	33	53
EIIIQRV	—	(exch) 0	53		HE, HE	20	73
ADEKNRT	KID, EYED	16	69		JUMPY	27	100
AELNPRT	REPLANT, HEP	80	149		NIX	30	130
EEINRTV	TREE, THE, RE	18	167		—	(exch) 0	130
EGILNUV	VEIN, TREEN	30	197		EXTENDED	69	199
CEGLNNU	JUNGLE	28	225		HOAR, HE, ON, AD, RE	35	234
ABCINRU	CRAB, CON, RAD, ARE	31	256		INDIANS, CRABS (challenged)	(chall) 0	234
GGIOSQU	GO, GU, ON	12	268		GAIN	10	244
AGIQSUW	SQUAW, GAINS	87	355		OI, ICON	8	252
CGIOSVW	VICE	18	373		GUM, UM	10	262
ADGORSW	AVOW	33	406		TR*ANSIT, SKID	77	339
DFGIORS	IF, OF	20	426		AUT*OS, AT	21	360
DGIOORS	WOODS	10	436		TO, TON	9	369
GIR		−5	431			5	374

Figure 45: A completed 2-player score-sheet,
showing moves, scores and running totals

Who Wins?

Quite simply, the game is won by the player finishing up with the highest number of points, after adjusting all opponents' scores to reflect unplayed tiles. The winner is not necessarily the player who goes out first, though going out does add to your points score. Near the end of a game where the scores are very close, going out first may make the difference between winning and not winning!

3

Words and Dictionaries

Allowable Words and Dictionaries

In the earlier section on challenges, it was explained that words are allowed if they can be found in an agreed standard dictionary, and they don't begin with an initial capital letter, are not marked as foreign, are not spelled with an apostrophe or hyphen, and are not abbreviations.

Dictionaries vary tremendously in the words they choose to include and exclude, as well as the way in which they treat the included words. Some dictionaries are only 'mini' or 'pocket' editions, containing a few thousand or tens of thousands of words. Dictionaries at the other end of the spectrum can be unabridged, containing several hundreds of thousands of words. In between these extremes are the concise editions, desktop editions, the collegiate editions and the 'shorter' dictionaries. (In this context, 'shorter' does not usually mean 'short' but 'shorter than unabridged'.)

Dictionaries place different emphases on different groups of words. Some treat obsolete and archaic words extensively, while others almost totally ignore them. Some attempt to be especially inclusive of scientific words. Some try to include all the words from the works of authors such as Shakespeare and Chaucer, while others only record a mere tip of the iceberg of these authors' words. Some dictionaries specialize in words from a particular part of the English-speaking world – Scotland, the USA, the Commonwealth, and so on.

Dictionaries are updated continuously. There are corrected and revised printings, new editions, and new dictionaries. Each tends to include a batch of new words, sometimes displacing some other batch of outmoded words. Depending on the age of your dictionary, it may or may not include specimens like DROOG, GLASNOST, GRUNGE, LASER and QUANGO.

Dictionaries vary in how they treat abbreviations. Some distinguish between abbreviations (such as BBC, PhD and YMCA) and shortened forms (such as BUS, PRAM and TRIKE), while others treat them all as abbreviations.

The message here is that you need to choose and agree your dictionary of authority before a game starts. It is no use hunting around in the middle of a game, once a word has been challenged, arguing that it may not be in this or that dictionary, but it might be in some other dictionary!

Chambers Dictionaries

Chambers dictionaries, in their various editions, have long been favourites of Scrabble players – as well as of crossword-puzzlers and word-puzzlers generally. As both *Chambers Twentieth Century Dictionary* and *Chambers 20th Century Dictionary*, up to and including the 1983 edition, Chambers has been *the* Scrabble reference dictionary for many years. A new edition was published in 1988, under the title of *Chambers English Dictionary*; this in turn was replaced in 1993 by, quite simply, *The Chambers Dictionary*.

The reason for the popularity of Chambers is not difficult to fathom. The various editions are each contained in a single volume, and are all reasonably compact. Chambers has always given comprehensive coverage to obsolete spellings and spellings found primarily in the works of authors such as Shakespeare, Spenser and Milton. Because of its Scottish origins, Chambers is also particularly strong on words from Scottish English.

As the preface to the current edition says:

> The comprehensiveness of its coverage commends Chambers as the dictionary for crosswords and other wordgames. It is the reference dictionary for the National Scrabble Championship, the National Scrabble Club Tournament and the National Scrabble Under-16 Championship. For those with competitive ambitions requiring word skills, it is the obvious choice , the width and character of its coverage being unrivalled by any other one-volume dictionary.

Official Scrabble Words

Although the various editions of Chambers dictionary served Scrabble players well over the years, there was always room for varying interpretations of the dictionary entries. Some typical instances are offered here, where there was scope for disagreement among Scrabble players.

While the verb forms (ending in -S, -ED and -ING) are usually straightforward to derive, there are instances where the derived forms are unclear. Although the dictionary lists the verb BINGE, it is not clear whether the present participle is spelled with or without an E – BINGING or BINGEING? Or perhaps both? For obsolete verbs, it could be quite difficult to work out what the appropriate derivative forms should be.

No one would argue with comparative and superlative forms of simple colours, such as BLUER and GREENEST, but what about similar forms of other colours? BEIGEST, ORANGER, PUCER, PURPLEST and the like. How can you tell whether these are valid or not?

What about plurals? No one would quibble with simple plurals such as DAYS, DESKS and DOMES, but there is plenty of scope for debate as to whether some nouns have plural forms at all – for example, NETBALL, OZONE and ZEAL. For some nouns, there is no question about the existence of a plural form, merely about how it is formed. Where the dictionary does not clearly indicate a plural form, Scrabble players could argue about the correct form. Should the plural be formed by the addition of an -S, -ES or -IES? Or is some more classically correct plural form appropriate? Or are both acceptable? Which is the correct plural form of a noun like SENARIUS? Is it SENARIUSES or SENARII, or maybe both? What is the correct plural of EAU? Is it EAUS or EAUX or both?

It is questions like these that led to the creation of Chambers' *Official Scrabble Words* (or OSW). First published in 1988, OSW is the definitive listing of allowable Scrabble words. It contains all valid words, their appropriate plurals, verb forms, comparatives and superlatives, and so on. All words are listed in strict alphabetical order, so that, for example, CAT and CATS are separated by over 200 other words beginning with CAT-. No definitions are given. If you need a definition, you should turn to the Chambers dictionary itself. The third edition of OSW, published mid-1994, is based on the most recent edition (1993) of *The Chambers Dictionary*. OSW contains approximately 150 000 words, more than enough for the most enthusiastic Scrabble player. Since its initial publication, OSW has been essential for Scrabble players and indispensable for those who have to adjudicate at organized Scrabble tournaments. It will also help to avoid family arguments in social games which come about through out-of-date dictionaries and misinterpretations about plurals, verb forms, and so on.

Official Scrabble Lists
Valuable and indispensable as *Official Scrabble Words* is, it merely presents words in strict alphabetic sequence. It does not provide a learning tool for Scrabble players. For example, what are the allowable four-letter words using a Z? What about six-letter words using a J? Which words are useful for offloading a clutch of awkward consonants? Are there any anagrams of CUTLERY? What words, if any, can be made from the letters AEINRSW? What words can be formed from ENOSTT and a blank?

It is to answer questions like these that you will need to turn to *Official Scrabble Lists* (or OSL). As the Introduction to OSL says:

> *Official Scrabble Lists* is a complete companion to *Official Scrabble Words*. OSL is a unique and thorough collection derived from the wealth of words within OSW and categorized into sections according to usefulness and interest ... The lists are an invaluable aid, acting as a convenient vocabulary-building guide for the newcomer and a specialist reference for the more experienced.

OSL presents numerous comprehensive lists, as well as many playing hints. The following selection of items from OSL's Contents page should serve to whet your appetite:

> 4-letter words
> Heavy words (those having many consonants)
> Awkward vowel dumps – U's
> Awkward consonant dumps – W's
> Q-words
> Words ending in -EST
> Words ending in -U
> The 6-plus-1 lists (seven-letter words created from common six-letter groups plus one other letter)
> The 6-plus-2 lists (eight-letter words created from common six-letter groups plus two other letters)

Hooks (those words which can be extended by the addition of one letter at the beginning or end)

7-letter anagrams

The Official Scrabble Players Dictionary

The American equivalent of the British OSW is *The Official Scrabble Players Dictionary* (OSPD for short). Published by Merriam-Webster, this volume contains all the allowable Scrabble words for use in North America. The OSPD lists plurals, verb forms, and comparatives and superlatives, in the same way as OSW, but it also contains very brief definitions. The OSPD is frequently updated, and it be can be quite difficult to determine whether two specific volumes are identical or slightly different, and which is the more recent if they are different. Although there is a considerable degree of overlap between OSW and the OSPD, there are many words which appear in only one of the two books. For this reason, the Scrabble World Championships rely on both OSW and OSPD. At the World Championships, a word is allowed if it appears in either of these two bibles. The OSPD is not available in Great Britain.

4

Playing Well

Introduction
Now that the rules, the scoring system and some of the basics of the game have been explained, you need to understand how to exploit these in order to play well. This chapter and the following ones go into the finer details of good play.

This chapter explains the importance of two-letter words. It reinforces some points about the high-, medium- and low-value tiles, as well as premium squares and bonuses. It discusses how to handle the Q, as well as the other big-scorers, the J, K, X and Z. The concepts of hooks, rack balancing, turnover, hooks and tile tracking are introduced. A shorthand notation for describing a play on the board is introduced. And the chapter finishes with some background on two different styles of play – playing for high scores and playing to win. Chapters 5 and 6 concentrate on putting all these points into action.

Two-letter Words

Two-letter words are extremely important in Scrabble, so much so that you ought to know all the valid ones. Although two-letter words occasionally score quite well, their main use is to allow you to play other words on the board at the same time, these other words contributing most of the points to a particular move. Sometimes a two-letter word will need to be played to open up your scoring opportunities for later in the game. You'll see shortly some examples of two-letter words being played.

Many newcomers to Scrabble tend to think that two-letter words are not allowed. There is no reason for this. The official rules have nothing to say about two-letter words. Words of this length are just as valid as those having three, four, five letters, and more. Other newcomers tend to think that two-letter words are restricted mainly to common everyday words, such as AM, BE, GO, IS and UP. Not so! A complete list of the two-letter words in *Official Scrabble Words* is given in Chapter 7. As you will see from the words in this list, there are many that are far from common. You need to be as familiar with words like AE, BA, GU, KY, OM and XU as you are with everyday ones. Even if you cannot commit all the unknown ones to memory at one attempt, you should try to learn a few at a time, until they are all second nature to you.

Here are some examples of two-letter words being played, demonstrating a number of different points.

In the first example, Figure 46, the word YODEL has already been played on the board. You may simply wish to get rid of an E from your rack, playing it beneath the Y, making the vertical word YE, and scoring a meagre 5 points.

In the next example, Figure 47, the words YODEL and OBOE are already on the board. You may find that you have a medium- or high-value letter tile on your rack, enabling you to score reasonably well from the 3L square adjacent to the initial O of OBOE. With an X on your rack, you might play OX for 25 points.

Figure 48 shows how you might make several two-letter words at the same time. The word WHITE is already on the board. By playing a two-letter word parallel to some of the existing letters, you will also make some other two-letter words. In this example, the word AN is played beneath the HI of WHITE, so making the vertical words HA and IN in the process. All three words (AN, HA and IN) will score points. In this example, AN scores 2 points, HA 5 points, and IN 2 points, for a total of 9 points.

Of course, you don't have to play only two tiles. Look at Figure 49. This time, instead of playing just AN, suppose you manage to play MEANER. This generates five two-letter words – WE, HA, IN, TE and ER – for a total of 29 points. (Do you agree? That's 12 for MEANER, 5 for WE, 5 for HA, 2 for IN, 3 for TE, and 2 for ER.) If you can make several two-letter words like this at the same turn, the points can start to mount up!

If you do play just two letters, then it can be beneficial to use a medium- or high-value tile in two of the words, one going across and one going down. Better still if the tile concerned covers a premium letter square. Look at the example in Figure

50. The word HOMEY is already on the board. Playing OW (it's one of the valid ones!) parallel to the ME of HOMEY, so that the W covers a 2L square, also creates the two-letter words OM and WE. (OM is another two-letter specimen you will need to get used to!) The score for this move is 22 points – 9 from OW, 4 from OM, and another 9 from WE. Notice how the W itself has contributed 16 of these points.

Sometimes you have to play a two-letter word in order to slot in on the board a word from your rack. Take a look at Figure 51. The words HOMEY, CHIMP and ACTED are already on the board. If you decide to play the word WRITE, you will need to place it so that the E is just above the A of ACTED, making the vertical word EA. Although EA only contributes 2 points, it has enabled you to slot in WRITE for its 24 points – making a total of 26 points for your turn.

In a similar fashion, you may find that you need to play a two-letter word in order to play all seven of your tiles down on the board. Remember how you score a 50-point bonus for using all seven of your tiles at the same turn. In the example shown in Figure 52, there are several words on the board already – HOLLY, KILOS, JEERS, YE, WHY, ELK, RODE and BREEZE. Suppose that you manage to spot the word RETAINS on your rack. In order to play this on the board, you have to make use of the E at the end of BREEZE, making the vertical word RE. Although RE only contributes 2 points and RETAINS 18 points, the real boost to your score comes from the 50-point bonus, making a total of 70 points on that turn.

Figure 53 shows an alternative place to play RETAINS, making the two-letter ER instead of RE. But this scores 1 point less – 3 points for ER, 16 points for RETAINS, and the 50-point bonus. 69 points in all. Although there is only a whisker of difference between the scores of these two moves, both are dependent on two-letter words.

The last two examples showed the use of two-letter words in enabling all seven of your letter tiles to be played, with only a very limited contribution from the two-letter words concerned. In this example, Figure 54, the use of two-letter words is still crucial to using all seven of your tiles, but the points scored by the four two-letter words help to increase your total score. The words already on the board are CREDO, ZOO, OX, ZIP, CRAMP,

GRAB, HEROIC, FOR and AYE. On your rack, you manage to see the seven-letter word RELAYED (as well as its anagrams DELAYER and LAYERED). Playing RELAYED above and parallel to HEROIC creates four two-letter words – AH, YE, ER and DO. RELAYED scores 38 points, the two-letter words score 23 points, and then there is the 50-point bonus. All for a total of 111 points! LAYERED could have been played in the same position, but scoring 90 points, while DELAYER would not have been playable.

It is quite often the case that you are close to having a seven-letter word on your rack, but there is nowhere to play it on the board. In this case, you might choose to play a two-letter word in order to create a position for an anticipated seven-letter word on your next turn. Take a look at the example in Figure 55. There are several words already on the board, but there is nowhere to put down RETAINS, which you spot on your rack again. Even its various anagrams (NASTIER, RETINAS and so on will not fit in anywhere.) What might you do? You might choose to play the simple word IT, scoring just 2 points. The paltry score here is almost irrelevant. What you are doing is holding back the letters AEINRS, hoping that the replacement tile you pick from the bag will enable you to play a seven-letter word at your next turn, turning IT into ITS. (Of course, your opponent is quite likely to realize what you are doing, and may decide to use IT or obstruct it at his next turn. The next two chapters will look at this kind of situation in more detail, discussing whether to make such openings, when to make them, what words to use, and so on.) For the time being, this example merely demonstrates another possible use of two-letter words.

Figure 46: Making the two-letter word YE

	A	B	C	D	E	F	G	H	I	J	K	L	M	N	O
1	3W			2L				3W				2L			3W
2		2W				3L				3L				2W	
3			2W				2L		2L				2W		
4	2L			2W				2L				2W			2L
5					2W						2W				
6		3L		**O**		3L				3L				3L	
7			2L	**B**			2L		2L				2L		
8	3W			**Y**	**O**	**D**	**E**	**L**				2L			3W
9			2L	**E**			2L		2L				2L		
10		3L				3L				3L				3L	

	A	B	C	D	E	F	G	H	I	J	K	L	M	N	O
1	3W			2L				3W				2L			3W
2		2W				3L				3L				2W	
3			2W				2L		2L				2W		
4	2L			2W				2L				2W			2L
5					2W						2W				
6		3L		**O**	**X**					3L				3L	
7			2L	**B**			2L		2L				2L		
8	3W			**Y**	**O**	**D**	**E**	**L**				2L			3W
9			2L	**E**			2L		2L				2L		
10		3L				3L				3L				3L	

Figure 47: Making the two-letter word OX

Figure 48: Making the two-letter words AN, HA and IN

Figure 49: Making the two-letter words WE, HA, IN, TE and ER

Figure 50: Making the two-letter words OW, OM and WE

Figure 51: Making the two-letter word EA

	A	B	C	D	E	F	G	H	I	J	K	L	M	N	O
1	3W			2L				3W				2L			3W
2		2W				3L				3L				2W	
3			B	R	E	E	Z	E	2L				2W		
4	2L			O				2L				2W			2L
5				D	2W						2W				
6		3L		E	L	K		W		3L				3L	
7			2L			I	2L	H	2L				2L		
8	3W			H	O	L	L	Y				2L			3W
9			2L			O	2L		2L				2L		
10		J	E	E	R	S				3L				3L	

	A	B	C	D	E	F	G	H	I	J	K	L	M	N	O
1	3W			2L				3W				2L			3W
2		2W				3L		R	E	T	A	I	N	S	
3			B	R	E	E	Z	E	2L				2W		
4	2L			O				2L				2W			2L
5				D	2W						2W				
6		3L		E	L	K		W		3L				3L	
7			2L			I	2L	H	2L				2L		
8	3W			H	O	L	L	Y				2L			3W
9			2L			O	2L		2L				2L		
10		J	E	E	R	S				3L				3L	

Figure 52: Making the two-letter word RE

	A	B	C	D	E	F	G	H	I	J	K	L	M	N	O
1	3W			2L				3W				2L			3W
2		2W				3L				3L				2W	
3			B	R	E	E	Z	E	2L				2W		
4	2L			O				R	E	T	A	I	N	S	2L
5				D	2W						2W				
6		3L		E	L	K		W		3L				3L	
7			2L			I	2L	H	2L				2L		
8	3W			H	O	L	L	Y				2L			3W
9			2L			O	2L		2L				2L		
10		J	E	E	R	S				3L				3L	

Figure 53: An alternative place for RETAINS

	A	B	C	D	E	F	G	H	I	J	K	L	M	N	O
1	3W			2L				3W				2L			3W
2		2W				3L				3L				2W	
3			2W		H	E	R	O	I	C			2W		
4	2L			2W				2L		R		2W			2L
5					2W			G	R	A	B				
6		3L			F	A	T			M				3L	
7			2L		O	Y	2L	Z	I	P			2L		
8	3W			C	R	E	D	O				2L			3W
9			2L				2L	O	X				2L		
10		3L				3L				3L				3L	

	A	B	C	D	E	F	G	H	I	J	K	L	M	N	O
1	3W			2L				3W				2L			3W
2		R	E	L	A	Y	E	D		3L				2W	
3			2W		H	E	R	O	I	C			2W		
4	2L			2W				2L		R		2W			2L
5					2W			G	R	A	B				
6		3L			F	A	T			M				3L	
7			2L		O	Y	2L	Z	I	P			2L		
8	3W			C	R	E	D	O				2L			3W
9			2L				2L	O	X				2L		
10		3L				3L				3L				3L	

Figure 54: Making the two-letter words AH, YE, ER and DO

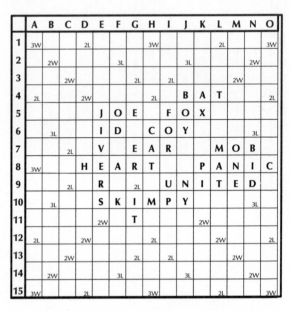

Figure 55: Making the two-letter word IT

By now, you should appreciate the value of two-letter words and understand the different ways in which they can be used. If you are still daunted by the number of unfamiliar two-letter words, try to learn a few every so often, and use them in your games whenever you get the opportunity. The more you use them, the more they will stick in your mind!

Premium Squares

In the earlier chapter on the basics of the game, the scoring effects of the various premium score squares were explained. You will recall that the light blue squares are double letter score squares, the dark blue ones are triple letter score squares, the pink ones are double word score squares, and the red ones are triple word score squares, abbreviated here as 2L, 3L, 2W and 3W squares. There were several examples given of the scoring effects of different combinations of premium squares.

Although it is rather obvious, you should try to use the premium squares when they are available for use. If you use a premium square, it will likely help you achieve a reasonable score for that turn, or maybe even a good score! It will also deny the opportunity to your opponent. After all, if you don't use a premium square, then your opponent might.

Try to make words going both ways through premium squares. This helps to double their effectiveness. Look at the simple example in Figure 56. Suppose you have an X on your rack, along with a mixture of other consonants and vowels. If you just play one tile, the X, on the 2L square to the right of the A in PENAL, then AX will score 17 points. But if you can make a word vertically as well, then the X doubled will score in both the horizontal and vertical words. In the example here, the word OX has been played. In addition to 17 points for AX, OX also scores 17 points, and NO another 2 points, giving you 36 points in all. Merely playing the extra tile, the O, has increased the score by a further 19 points – over 100%!

The effect is similar if there is a 3L square which can be exploited in this way. Look at the example shown in Figure 57. The words YEOMEN and CREAM are already on the board. Notice the 3L square adjacent to the E of CREAM. You might be able to play OH vertically, also making the words OR and HE. The point value of the H is tripled in both the words it appears in, OH and HE. This move scores 28 points. Compare this with the 13 point score you would have got if you had played just the H. Putting the O down with the H has boosted the score from 13 to 28 points.

Figure 58 shows the impact of using a couple of 2L squares where words go in both directions through each of the squares. Suppose you are able to play an H and Y around the A of CZAR. You have made three words – HAY, HEN and YE. In HAY, the H and Y are both doubled; in HEN, the H is doubled; and in YE, the Y is doubled. This scores 36 points, not bad for two tiles!

Watch out, too, for the cumulative effect of a 3L square and a 2W square. Look at the example in Figure 59. The relatively modest word TORCH can be played with great effect if the H covers the 3L square above the E of EBONY. TORCH scores 36 points, and HE adds a further 13 points, for a total score of 49 points. Notice that the number of points contributed by the H is 36, almost two-thirds of the score for the entire move!

Even where you are not able to use the 2W squares in conjunction with premium letter score squares (the 2L and 3L ones), do try and make use of them if you can incorporate a high-value tile, perhaps already on the board, into your move. Look at the example in Figure 60. Even if you only have low-value tiles on your rack, you might be able to make use of the X already on the board. If you can incorporate that into a word covering a 2W square, you are squeezing value out of tiles already on the board. INDEX, for example, scores 26 points – not a bad score for playing just I, N and D.

You may occasionally see a letter sitting part way between two 2W squares. Try to find a word which covers both these squares. By covering two 2W squares together you effectively quadruple the point values of the tiles in your word. You can get some quite hefty scores in this way, even if you don't play all seven of your tiles. The example in Figure 61 shows how the letters of BATING can be positioned around the H, covering two 2W squares. The point value of the tiles in BATHING is only 13 points, but quadrupled, that scores a very healthy 52 points! Do watch out for opportunities like this.

If you can spot a move reaching one of the 3W squares, do look carefully to see what use you can make of it. Even quite short words can produce good scores once you triple their point values. In the example shown in Figure 62, the K of KING has opened up the 3W square in the top left-hand corner. Almost any word using the K and reaching that red corner square will be worth a good few points. The solution shown, making the word PINK, notches up a useful 30 points. If you had played a longer word, or one with a higher point value, the score could have been markedly better.

The example in Figure 61 urged you to be on the lookout for moves going through two 2W squares. Even better than these are moves which allow you to cover two 3W squares. The example shown in Figure 63 builds on the word EACH, already on the board. Simply playing the four letters BLES around EACH will produce a fantastic 135 points! These sorts of opportunities are few and far between. Take them if and when they arise. And conversely, try not to set up such possibilities for your opponent. (In the chapter on playing for high scores, you will learn the whys and wherefores of deliberately opening up such possibilities.)

Sometimes the pattern of words on the board enables you to make two words which both cover the same 2W square. You need to appreciate the value of such openings. The example in Figure 64 shows how the word RING occurs just to the right of a 2W square. RING cries out to be turned into BRING or WRING. If you can also make a word vertically through that same 2W square, then you will see the effect of the 2W square applied to both words. The example here shows the word WHIM being played vertically. It this example, WRING is worth 18 points, and WHIM is worth 24 points. MA, a by-product of the move, adds a further 4 points, for a grand total of 46 points.

In the same vein, if you can use a 3W square in words going horizontally and vertically, then that is well worth considering. Figure 65 shows PINE being turned into OPINE, with the vertical word ODE being played. The three modest tiles O, D and E have generated an impressive 38 points. A longer word, or perhaps one beginning with SH, SP or ST would have raked in even more points!

	A	B	C	D	E	F	G	H	I	J	K	L	M	N	O
1	3W			2L				3W				2L			3W
2		2W				3L				3L				2W	
3			2W					2L		2L				2W	
4	2L			2W				P				2W			2L
5					2W			E			2W				
6		3L				3L		N		3L				3L	
7			2L					A	2L				2L		
8	3W			2L				L				2L			3W
9			2L						2L				2L		
10		3L				3L				3L				3L	

	A	B	C	D	E	F	G	H	I	J	K	L	M	N	O
1	3W			2L				3W				2L			3W
2		2W				3L				3L				2W	
3			2W					2L		2L				2W	
4	2L			2W				P				2W			2L
5					2W			E			2W				
6		3L				3L		N	O	3L				3L	
7			2L					A	X				2L		
8	3W			2L				L				2L			3W
9			2L						2L				2L		
10		3L				3L				3L				3L	

Figure 56: Using a 2L square in two directions

	A	B	C	D	E	F	G	H	I	J	K	L	M	N	O
1	3W			2L				3W				2L			3W
2		2W				3L				3L				2W	
3			2W				2L		2L				2W		
4	2L			2W		C		2L				2W			2L
5					2W	R					2W				
6		3L				E				3L				3L	
7			2L			A	2L		2L				2L		
8	3W		Y	E	O	M	E	N				2L			3W
9			2L				2L		2L				2L		
10		3L				3L				3L				3L	

	A	B	C	D	E	F	G	H	I	J	K	L	M	N	O
1	3W			2L				3W				2L			3W
2		2W				3L				3L				2W	
3			2W				2L		2L				2W		
4	2L			2W		C		2L				2W			2L
5					O	R					2W				
6		3L			H	E				3L				3L	
7			2L			A	2L		2L				2L		
8	3W		Y	E	O	M	E	N				2L			3W
9			2L				2L		2L				2L		
10		3L				3L				3L				3L	

Figure 57: Using a 3L square in two directions

	A	B	C	D	E	F	G	H	I	J	K	L	M	N	O
1	3W			2L				C				2L			3W
2		2W				3L		Z		3L				2W	
3			2W				2L	A	2L				2W		
4	2L			2W	W	H	E	R	E			2W			2L
5			A	L	I	E	N				2W				
6		3L			D	3L				3L				3L	
7			2L		E		2L		2L				2L		
8	3W			P	R	I	M	E				2L			3W
9			2L				2L		2L				2L		
10		3L				3L				3L				3L	

	A	B	C	D	E	F	G	H	I	J	K	L	M	N	O
1	3W			2L				C				2L			3W
2		2W				3L		Z		3L				2W	
3			2W				H	A	Y				2W		
4	2L			2W	W	H	E	R	E			2W			2L
5			A	L	I	E	N				2W				
6		3L			D	3L				3L				3L	
7			2L		E		2L		2L				2L		
8	3W			P	R	I	M	E				2L			3W
9			2L				2L		2L				2L		
10		3L				3L				3L				3L	

Figure 58: Using 2L squares, each in two directions

	A	B	C	D	E	F	G	H	I	J	K	L	M	N	O
1	3W			2L				3W				2L			3W
2		2W				3L			3L					2W	
3			2W			E	B	O	N	Y			2W		
4	2L			2W			O	X				2W			2L
5				T	2W		B	Y			2W				
6		3L		O		3L		G	3L				3L		
7			2L	A			H	E	M			2L			
8	3W			D	R	A	I	N				2L			3W
9			2L				P		2L			2L			
10		3L				3L			3L				3L			

	A	B	C	D	E	F	G	H	I	J	K	L	M	N	O
1	3W			2L				3W				2L			3W
2		T	O	R	C	H			3L					2W	
3			2W			E	B	O	N	Y			2W		
4	2L			2W			O	X				2W			2L
5				T	2W		B	Y			2W				
6		3L		O		3L		G	3L				3L		
7			2L	A			H	E	M			2L			
8	3W			D	R	A	I	N				2L			3W
9			2L				P		2L			2L			
10		3L				3L			3L				3L			

Figure 59: Using a combination of 3L and 2W squares

	A	B	C	D	E	F	G	H	I	J	K	L	M	N	O
1	3W			2L				3W				2L			3W
2		2W				3L				3L				2W	
3			2W				W	E	2L				2W		
4	2L			2W			E	X				2W			2L
5					2W			O			2W				
6		3L				3L		D	R	Y				3L	
7			2L		M		2L	U	2L				2L		
8	3W			J	U	M	P	S				2L			3W
9			B	O	G		2L		2L				2L		
10		3L		Y		3L				3L				3L	

	A	B	C	D	E	F	G	H	I	J	K	L	M	N	O
1	3W			2L				3W				2L			3W
2		2W				3L				3L				2W	
3			2W				W	E	2L				2W		
4	2L			I	N	D	E	X				2W			2L
5					2W			O			2W				
6		3L				3L		D	R	Y				3L	
7			2L		M		2L	U	2L				2L		
8	3W			J	U	M	P	S				2L			3W
9			B	O	G		2L		2L				2L		
10		3L		Y		3L				3L				3L	

Figure 60: Using a 2W square

Figure 61: Using two 2W squares

	A	B	C	D	E	F	G	H	I	J	K	L	M	N	O
1	3W			2L				3W				2L			3W
2		2W				3L				3L				2W	
3			2W			2L		2L					2W		
4	K	I	N	G				2L				2W			2L
5				R	E					2W					
6		3L		O	X	3L	T	R	I	M				3L	
7			2L	O		P	O	2L				2L			
8	3W			V	Y	I	N	G				2L			3W
9			2L	E		T	E	2L				2L			
10		3L				3L				3L				3L	

	A	B	C	D	E	F	G	H	I	J	K	L	M	N	O
1	P			2L				3W				2L			3W
2	I	2W				3L				3L				2W	
3	N		2W			2L		2L					2W		
4	K	I	N	G				2L				2W			2L
5				R	E					2W					
6		3L		O	X	3L	T	R	I	M				3L	
7			2L	O		P	O	2L				2L			
8	3W			V	Y	I	N	G				2L			3W
9			2L	E		T	E	2L				2L			
10		3L				3L				3L				3L	

Figure 62: Using a 3W square

	A	B	C	D	E	F	G	H	I	J	K	L	M	N	O
1	3W		E	A	C	H		3W				2L			3W
2		2W	A		R	3L			3L				2W		
3			T	R	A	M	P		2L				2W		
4	2L		E	2W	Z	O		V				2W			2L
5			N		Y	U		I		2W					
6		3L				N		T	A	X				3L	
7			2L			T	2L	A	2L				2L		
8	3W			J	U	S	T	L	Y			2L			3W
9			2L			2L		2L					2L		
10		3L				3L			3L					3L	

	A	B	C	D	E	F	G	H	I	J	K	L	M	N	O
1	B	L	E	A	C	H	E	S				2L			3W
2		2W	A		R	3L			3L				2W		
3			T	R	A	M	P		2L				2W		
4	2L		E	2W	Z	O		V				2W			2L
5			N		Y	U		I		2W					
6		3L				N		T	A	X				3L	
7			2L			T	2L	A	2L				2L		
8	3W			J	U	S	T	L	Y			2L			3W
9			2L			2L		2L					2L		
10		3L				3L			3L					3L	

Figure 63: Using two 3W squares

	A	B	C	D	E	F	G	H	I	J	K	L	M	N	O
1	3W			2L				3W				2L			3W
2		2W		D		3L				3L				2W	
3			2W	R	I	N	G		2L				2W		
4	2L			2W	R		L	E	T	T	E	R			2L
5		M	I	N	K		A		W	I	N				
6		3L		A		3L	Z	O	O	3L				3L	
7			2L	R			E	H	2L				2L		
8	3W			Y			D	O				2L			3W
9			2L			2L			2L				2L		
10		3L				3L				3L				3L	

	A	B	C	D	E	F	G	H	I	J	K	L	M	N	O
1	3W			2L				3W				2L			3W
2		2W		D		3L				3L				2W	
3			W	R	I	N	G		2L				2W		
4	2L		H	2W	R		L	E	T	T	E	R			2L
5		M	I	N	K		A		W	I	N				
6		3L	M	A		3L	Z	O	O	3L				3L	
7			2L	R			E	H	2L				2L		
8	3W			Y			D	O				2L			3W
9			2L			2L			2L				2L		
10		3L				3L				3L				3L	

Figure 64: Using a 2W square in two directions

	A	B	C	D	E	F	G	H	I	J	K	L	M	N	O
1	3W	P	I	N	E			3W			C	2L			3W
2		O	N	E		3L				J	O			2W	
3			D				2L	N	A	B		2W			
4	2L		E	M	I	T		2L	U	P		2W			2L
5			X	I	2W	A				E	2W				
6		3L		T		K	N	O	T	S				3L	
7			O	R		E	2L	D	2L				2L		
8	3W		W	E		N		E				2L			3W
9			N				2L		2L				2L		
10		3L				3L				3L				3L	

	A	B	C	D	E	F	G	H	I	J	K	L	M	N	O
1	O	P	I	N	E			3W			C	2L			3W
2	D	O	N	E		3L				J	O			2W	
3	E		D				2L	N	A	B		2W			
4	2L		E	M	I	T		2L	U	P		2W			2L
5			X	I	2W	A				E	2W				
6		3L		T		K	N	O	T	S				3L	
7			O	R		E	2L	D	2L				2L		
8	3W		W	E		N		E				2L			3W
9			N				2L		2L				2L		
10		3L				3L				3L				3L	

Figure 65: Using a 3W square in two directions

These few examples show how scores can mount up quite dramatically from careful and considered use of premium score squares. Don't just look for a word on your rack and then plonk it down anywhere on the board. Study the board carefully. What premium score squares are accessible? Look for places to play words that will score well. Having found one or some possible places, then look at the letters on your rack to see which tiles can be used to cover the chosen premium squares. Of course, in using up certain premium squares, you may well be opening up others for your opponent. But more of that later!

The High-value Letters
The five tiles worth 5 or more points can be regarded as the high-value letters. They are:

J   8 points
K   5 points
Q   10 points
X   8 points
Z   10 points

Try not to squander these letters! When you get any of these letters on your rack, try to squeeze as many points from them as you can. Try to use them in conjunction with premium squares. If you can play them in conjunction with more than one premium square, so much the better. If you can get a high-value letter on a 3L square and the word played also covers a 2W square, you will be multiplying the face value of that letter by 6. Similarly, watch out for 2L squares which can be used in conjunction with 3W squares. The ultimate possibility is to get one of these high-value letters on a 2L square where the word played covers two 3W squares! In this case, you could be multiplying the face value of the letter by 18!

In trying to spot words using these high-value letters, try to bear in mind the sorts of sequences that they occur in. There aren't many of these, but do look out for words beginning EX- and QU-, or words using the -CK- and -NK- sequences, or words ending in -IZE and -QUE.

	A		F	G	H	I	J	K	L	M	N	O
1	3W				3W				2L			3W
2			3L				3L	P			2W	
3				2L		2L		A		2W		
4	2L				2L			N	2W			2L
5								S				
6			3L				K	I	D		3L	
7				2L		2L		E		2L		
8	3W			C	E	N	T	S	2L			3W
9				A		2L				2L		
10			3L	B	E		3L				3L	
11								2W				

	A		F	G	H	I	J	K	L	M	N	O
1	3W				3W				2L			3W
2			3L			E	X	P	O	R	T	
3				2L		2L		A		2W		
4	2L				2L			N	2W			2L
5								S				
6			3L				K	I	D		3L	
7				2L		2L		E		2L		
8	3W			C	E	N	T	S	2L			3W
9				A		2L				2L		
10			3L	B	E		3L				3L	
11								2W				

Figure 66: Scoring 62 points with the X

In Figure 66, the words CENTS, CAB, BE, PANSIES and KID are already on the board. With the letters EFIORTX on your rack, there are several scoring opportunities. You could play any of:

> IBEX across from F10, for 15 points;
> EXERT down from H8, for 21 points;
> TAXI across from J3, for 22 points;
> FOXIER across from H11, for 37 points.

But don't overlook the 3L square at J2. If you could find a word with the X on that square, using the P of PANSIES, and covering the 2W square at N2, that would score well over 50 points! EXPORT is the word you need to spot, scoring 62 points, of which the X alone has contributed 48 points.

Watch out for possibilities of playing a high-value letter on a premium square that is used in both horizontal and vertical words. In Figure 67, the words THETA, TAME, VET, CAM, TAIL, HER and YELP are already on the board. Your rack is comprised of EINOSWX. Some of the possibilities available to you are:

> OXER down from L3, for 27 points;
> SIX across from K9, for 28 points;
> NIXES down from M3, for 33 points;
> PIXES or POXES across from K8, for 45 points.

But consider the 3L square at J10. You could play OXEN down from the J9 square, making VETO, TAX, CAME and EN at the same time, scoring a very healthy 70 points.

	A	B		F	G	H	I	J	K	L	M	N	O
1	3W					3W				2L			3W
2		2W		3L				3L				2W	
3					2L		2L				2W		
4	2L					2L				2W			2L
5									Y				
6		3L		3L			H	E	R			3L	
7					2L	T	A	I	L		2L		
8	3W					H			P	2L			3W
9					V	E	T				2L		
10		3L		3L		T	A	3L				3L	
11					C	A	M		2W				
12	2L					2L	E			2W			2L
13					2L		2L				2W		
14		2W		3L				3L				2W	
15	3W					3W				2L			3W

	A	B		F	G	H	I	J	K	L	M	N	O
1	3W					3W				2L			3W
2		2W		3L				3L				2W	
3					2L		2L				2W		
4	2L					2L				2W			2L
5									Y				
6		3L		3L			H	E	R			3L	
7					2L	T	A	I	L		2L		
8	3W					H			P	2L			3W
9					V	E	T	O			2L		
10		3L		3L		T	A	X				3L	
11					C	A	M	E	2W				
12	2L					2L	E	N		2W			2L
13					2L		2L				2W		
14		2W		3L				3L				2W	
15	3W					3W				2L			3W

Figure 67: Scoring 70 points with the X

Some board positions offer the possibility of plays that are a combination of those just seen, involving a word in one direction that uses both 3L and 2W squares, as well as a perpendicular word using a 3L square. In Figure 68, the words HERE, PENNIES, ARIAS and BIKE are already on the board. With the letters AELRUWX on your rack, you could play:

> AX down from I10, for 20 points;
> WAX across from F9, for 29 points;
> WAX down from F12, for 29 points;
> WAX down from F8, for 40 points.

But watch out for the 3L square at F14. If you could make a five- or six-letter word, covering the 2W square at B14, that would really score well. RELAX across from B14 fits the bill, and nets 81 points.

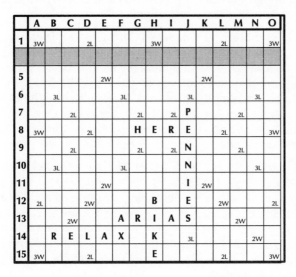

Figure 68: Scoring 81 points with the X

Handling the Q!

Although the Q is one of the five high-value letters, it is worth a paragraph to itself on how to handle it properly. The problem with the Q is that it usually requires a U in order to play it. Once upon a time, a Q could be considered unplayable without a corresponding U. But with the advent of various foreign words into dictionaries, a small collection of words having a Q but no U has become available to Scrabble players. The unplayableness of the Q has diminished over the years, and will continue to do so.

The 1972 edition of *Chambers Twentieth Century Dictionary* contained no words beginning with a Q which wasn't followed by a U. For all intents and purposes, if you had the Q but no U, you were stuck. You either had to retain the Q until a U appeared on your rack or in an accessible position on the board, or you had to exchange the Q, hoping that your opponent would pick it up, although you often found it returning to your own rack three or four moves letter. Frustration!

The 1983 edition of *Chambers 20th Century Dictionary* saw the introduction of words such as QADI, QANAT, QIBLA, QINTAR and SUQ. (SUQ is included here, because, although it has a U, it also lacks the vowel which usually follows the QU combination.) Scrabble players avidly learned these words. There were now some ways of using the Q without the normally requisite U. QADI was probably the new Q word most often used.

Five years on, the 1988 edition of *Chambers English Dictionary* introduced QAT, QIGONG, QWERTY and TALAQ. The advent of QAT as an allowable Scrabble word immediately saw it as the most frequently played Q word. All you needed to play your Q was an A on the board and a T on your rack, or vice versa. QAT was often played for 12 points, although sometimes many more. 12 points was better than exchanging the Q and not scoring anything!

The 1993 edition of *The Chambers Dictionary* has added a few more specimens to the list. There's QASIDA, QI, QIVIUT and QOPH. QIVIUT is not very useful, because it still requires a U. The word in this list which has dramatically reduced the Q's difficulty factor is QI. With nine I's in a set, the likelihood of an

I on your rack or an available I somewhere on the board is quite high. Just as it has long been possible to score 62 points by playing the Z (making ZO in two directions, with the Z on a 3L square), so it is now possible to pick up the same score by playing just the Q. QI both vertically and horizontally, with the Q on a 3L square, racks up 62 points also!

Although the emergence of QI (and its plural QIS) has seriously diminished the difficulties long associated with the Q, it is probably still worth airing the sort of considerations that previous generations of Scrabble players wrestled with, and which may still be appropriate today, if the likes of QAT, QADI and QI aren't playable.

When you find yourself picking a Q from the bag of unused tiles, check to see how many U's have already been played on the board. If there is a U on the board that can be used for a reasonable score, then by all means you should seriously consider using it, although keep an eye out for possibilities like QADI, QAT and QI.

What you shouldn't do is hang on to the Q for turn after turn, hoping that a U or a blank or an I (for QI) or an AT (for QAT) will turn up. If you have those letters when you pick up the Q, by all means consider playing off the Q on your next turn. But all the while you are hanging on to the Q concentrating on your next pickup of letters, the chances are you won't be scoring well in the meantime, and your opponent will be streaking ahead of you on points.

If you have the Q but no U, no blank, no I, or no AT, consider exchanging the Q. This might be an opportunity where you could return other unwanted letters to the unused pool – perhaps a V, maybe some duplicate vowels. But do beware. Putting the Q back gives your opponent an almost 50% chance of getting it, and he may well be able to score well from it. After all, if you haven't got the necessary U, blank, I or AT, he may well have! Exchanging the Q – now that it is so much easier to use than 10 or 20 years ago – may well be giving your opponent the chance of a big score. Of course, if you pick up the Q on a later turn, you may just have wasted a turn. Think carefully before returning the Q.

Of course, your handling of the Q will be greatly improved if you have an extensive knowledge of the shorter words using a Q. Experienced Scrabble players will know most – if not all – of the Q words with three, four and five letters. Having a U to go with your Q will not automatically solve your Q problems. Knowing everyday words such as QUEEN, QUITE and QUOTA may not be sufficient. You should arm yourself with the likes of QUAIR, QUEME, QUINE and QUOLL. And don't overlook the likes of BURQA, QUALIA, QUYTED and INQILAB. You will find all the allowable Q words listed alphabetically and by length in *Official Scrabble Lists*.

Handling the J, K, X and Z

Although having one or more of these letters on your rack won't involve you in the same considerations as the Q, nevertheless, you will need to have a good knowledge of the three-, four- and five-letter words using these letters. Useful as they are, words like AJAR, NAKED, EXITED and ZANIEST will need to be supplemented with more exotic specimens – for example, DOJO, KRENG, EXILIC and TAILZIE. You will find all the allowable J, X and Z words – although not all of the K ones – listed alphabetically and by length in *Official Scrabble Lists*.

The Medium-value Letters

The tiles with a face-value of 3 or 4 points can be regarded as the medium-value letters.

There are 18 of these tiles, distributed like this:

2 B's	3 points	2 H's	4 points	2 V's	4 points
2 C's	3 points	2 M's	3 points	2 W's	4 points
2 F's	4 points	2 P's	3 points	2 Y's	4 points

The advice given for the high-value letters applies also to these medium-value letters, although with slightly less force. Because of their lower point values, the effect of playing one of these tiles on a premium square will be less marked than that of playing a high-value letter. Watch out especially for an H or a Y on your rack. These can be particularly useful for scoring well.

Watch out for common letter sequences in which these letters occur. Here are some of the commoner ones:

ACC-	-IVE	SC-	-TCH
-CH	-MP	SCH-	-TH-
-FF	-NCH	SM-	TW-
-GHT	-PPY	SP-	-VED
-IFY	-RCH	SW-	WH-

In Figure 69, the words PRISM, SERRATED, ICY, LATHE, WOMEN and BARONS are already on the board. You have ABEHLOW on your rack. Possible plays include:

LAH down from G11, for 21 points;
WHOA down from J1, for 24 points;
WHOLE down from M2, for 28 points;
HOBBLE across from I3, for 34 points.

But best of all is the play of a vertical word through the 3L square at J6. Thus, BAH or BOH down from J4, scoring 40 points.

In Figure 70, the words ARROW, HARK, HAIR, EX and WADDLE are already on the board. With the letters AEGMMSY on your rack, what plays are possible? Some of the possibilities are:

MY down from G8, for 22 points;
SHARK down from J5, for 22 points;
GAMEY across from I13, for 26 points;
GAMES down from N2, for 30 points.

However, don't overlook the fact that HAIR can have a Y added to become HAIRY. Is there a five- or six-letter word ending in Y which will cover the 2W square at N2? GAMMY is the obvious possibility, although GEMMY also exists. Played down from N2, either of these would score 61 points.

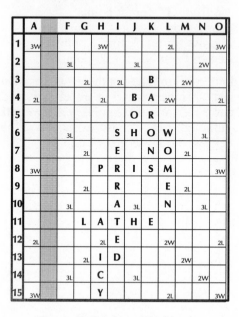

Figure 69: Scoring well with an H

	A		F	G	H	I	J	K	L	M	N	O
1	3W				3W				2L			3W
2			3L				3L				2W	
3				2L		2L				2W		
4	2L				2L				2W			2L
5							E	X				
6			3L				H	A	I	R	3L	
7				2L		2L		A		2L		
8	3W				A	R	R	O	W			3W
9				2L		2L		K	A	2L		
10			3L				3L		D		3L	
11								2W	D			
12	2L				2L				L			2L
13				2L		2L			E	2W		
14			3L				3L				2W	
15	3W				3W				2L			3W

	A		F	G	H	I	J	K	L	M	N	O
1	3W				3W				2L			3W
2			3L				3L				G	
3				2L		2L				2W	A	
4	2L				2L				2W		M	2L
5							E	X			M	
6			3L				H	A	I	R	Y	
7				2L		2L		A		2L		
8	3W				A	R	R	O	W			3W
9				2L		2L		K	A	2L		
10			3L				3L		D		3L	
11								2W	D			
12	2L				2L				L			2L
13				2L		2L			E	2W		
14			3L				3L				2W	
15	3W				3W				2L			3W

Figure 70: Scoring well with a Y

The Low-value Letters
There are 75 tiles with a face value of 1 or 2 points. They are distributed like this:

9 A's	9 I's	6 R's
4 D's	4 L's	4 S's
12 E's	6 N's	6 T's
3 G's	8 O's	4 U's

In addition, there are the two blank tiles, each with a face value of 0 points. All told, that's a full 77 tiles worth 2 or less points. These are the tiles which you can expect to have on your rack time after time. Not all your racks can be chock-full of high- and medium-value letters, and, indeed, you shouldn't want them to be. By themselves, the low-value tiles will not tend to score highly. Their usefulness comes in several ways, though.

You will need to use these tiles in conjunction with the high- and medium-value letters. After all, there are very few words that are composed solely of high- and medium-value letters. In the last five scoring examples, shown in Figures 66-70, the highest scores were obtained with the words EXPORT, OXEN, RELAX, BOH and GAMMY. You will invariably have to use your low-value letters to achieve the sorts of scores involved in these examples.

50-point Bonuses
Playing well requires you to achieve the occasional 50-point bonus for playing out all seven of your tiles in one go. Bonuses have been referred to in several of the previous sections. But what do you need to do so that your seven tiles do make a word?

50-point Bonuses Using the Low-value Letters
Racks with a good mix of low-value letters are more likely to lead to bonus words than those with a surfeit of high- and medium-value letters. Remember that bonus words bring you an extra 50 points, and so are what you need to score well. The extreme example is the seven-letter group AEINRST. The seven letters alone give rise to 10 different words – thus:

ANESTRI	NASTIER	RATINES	RESIANT	RETAINS
RETINAS	RETSINA	STAINER	STARNIE	STEARIN

Notice that phrase 'good mix'. If you have a rack with all low-value letters, you will find them more malleable if you don't have duplicate letters. With the exception of E's, S's and blanks, you will tend to find that two or more of any particular letter will make your rack of seven tiles less likely to form a bonus word. Of course, this isn't always the case, but it is a good general rule of thumb. If you have a rack with duplicate A's or I's or N's or R's, try to use up the duplicate letters. You may have to accept a lowish score to do this, but this is more likely to put you en route for a bonus word than continuing to hold duplicate letters on your rack. More of this subject – rack balancing – a little later on.

In searching for bonus words using the low-value letters, do bear in mind the common letter sequences. Some of the more obvious ones are listed here:

-AL	-ER	-IES	-ION	-OUS
-ANT	-ERS	-IEST	-IST	OUT-
-ATE	-EST	-ILE	-ITE	RE-
-ATOR	-IAL	IN-	-LE	-TLE
-ED	-IAN	-INE	-OR	UN-
-ENT	-IER	-ING	-OUR	-URE

50-point Bonuses Using the Medium-value and High-value Letters
Bonus words are not always made up from the low-value letters. In real Scrabble games, many a bonus word uses the medium-value and high-value letters. You will often find that one of the medium- and high-value letters will combine well with the low-value letters in order to make a bonus word. Here are some typical examples of such bonus words:

ANTIQUE	GLEAMED	NERVOUS	TUXEDOS
BRAISED	HEADSET	OBTAINS	UPRATED
CANDIES	JETTIES	PIRATES	VERSION
DEFEATS	KNITTED	QUARTER	WEEDING
EVINCES	LEAVING	REQUITE	YEARNED
FAIREST	MAIDENS	SHEARED	ZESTIER

Less frequently, you will see bonus words played which use two or more of the medium- and high-value letters. A bonus word using two of these letters isn't so rare, perhaps. However, you are unlikely to see words with as many as five of them. Two lists follow. The words in the left-hand list use only two of the medium- and high-value tiles, and may well be seen occasionally on Scrabble boards. The words in the right-hand list use three or more of the medium- and high-value letters, and are unlikely to be played much.

ANCHORS	BUXOMER
BRISKET	COMPANY
CONJURE	DIMMISH
EXPORTS	EXAMPLE
HARPIES	FUCHSIA
HERBIST	HAWKERS
INJECTS	ICHABOD
MOBSTER	JUSTIFY
PINKEST	MYSTIFY
SWIFTER	PHALANX
THRIVES	QUARTZY
WREATHS	TWITCHY
ZITHERS	ZYTHUMS

Some Terminology Explained

Subsequent chapters will go into further detail on how to apply the basic rules and the points already covered in this chapter. In order to do this, you need to be introduced to some terminology used by good Scrabble players. The concepts are quite simple, but they do need explaining so that they can be conveniently referred to in the later chapters. The concepts and terms that you need to be aware of are hooks, rack balancing, turnover, tile tracking, and a kind of shorthand notation for documenting moves. Each of these is now explained.

Hooks

A hook is, quite simply, a word which can have a single letter added to it, at either end, to create a new word. Such words provide convenient places for other words to hook on to, perpendicular to the original word. The simplest form of hook is the addition of an -S to create the plural form of a noun (for example, DOOR to DOORS, PINT to PINTS) or the -S derivative of a verb (for example, SAY to SAYS, GLOAT to GLOATS).

Of course, there are many possibilities other than just the -S ones. Most letters are capable of being hooked on to the end of an appropriate base word. Here are some other hook words that can have letters added at the end to create new words:

SAG(A)	TAX(I)	TIN(T)
HER(B)	BAR(K)	MEN(U)
MANIA(C)	PEAR(L)	GO(V)
TEN(D)	WAR(M)	VIE(W)
COP(E)	WAR(N)	CHATEAU(X)
GOO(F)	HER(O)	BULL(Y)
PAN(G)	CAR(P)	QUART(Z)
BAT(H)	LOVE(R)	

All the hook words offered so far have involved the addition of a letter at the end of a word. However, letters can be added to the beginning of words as well. Simple examples are HARK to SHARK and RIPE to TRIPE. Most letters are capable of being hooked on to the beginning of an appropriate base word. Here are some other hook words that can have letters added at the beginning to create new words:

(A)CORN	(J)ANGLE	(S)PLAY
(B)RIGHT	(K)ILL	(T)HERE
(C)LIMB	(L)INK	(U)SING
(D)RAG	(M)INK	(V)ALE
(E)STATE	(N)EARLY	(W)HEN
(F)LIP	(O)PEN	(Y)ELL
(G)LISTEN	(P)RANG	(Z)ANY
(H)ARK	(R)ATE	

Some words provide multiple hook possibilities. For example, a simple word like EAR can have several letters added at the front (B, D, F, G, H, L, N, P, R, S, T, W, Y), as well as several letters at the end (D, L, N, S).

You will need to gain a knowledge of what letters can be added to which words. This is especially important in converting two-letter words to three-letter ones, 'the two-to-three hooks', although it is useful to know many of the three-to-four hooks, and even some of the longer ones.

While it is important to know what letters can be added to words already on the board, it is also important to know the hook words to be played in the first place. There are occasions when you will want to play a hook word, knowing full well it can be added to later in the game, potentially offering a place to play a bonus word! But, equally, there are occasions when it is valuable to play a word which you know isn't a hook word, thereby denying your opponent the possibility of adding to it!

Rack Balancing
The concept of rack balancing has nothing to do with trying to balance your rack on your knees because of lack of space! It is simply the idea of trying to keep two or three vowels on your rack, and four or five consonants. If your hand is top-heavy with consonants (say, ABDGHLM), you will have relatively few options about what to play when your next turn comes round. Similarly, with too many vowels on your rack (perhaps ACEIOOU) your choices will be restricted. Discounting the two blanks and the two Y's (which can function as consonants and vowels), there are 42 vowels in a Scrabble set, and 54 consonants. The more balanced you keep your rack, the greater the chance will be of good-scoring possibilities available to you, either as bonus words or as shorter but good-scoring moves.

With a selection of tiles such as ABDGHLM, you should strive to play off as many of the consonants as you can, possibly making use of a vowel already on the board, thereby retaining your single vowel. Words that spring to mind are BALM, GLAM and LAMB – or, using a vowel already on the board, GAMBOL, GOLD and LIMB. On average you will pick up vowels and consonants in the ratio of five to four, so you should always be striving to get an unbalanced rack back to a balanced state.

Turnover
Turnover is merely the number of tiles you use on a particular play. The greater your turnover, the greater your chances of picking up the remaining good tiles (perhaps a blank, or an S, or maybe the X or Z), thereby denying them to your opponent. If you have an unbalanced rack of letters, you should strive for a high turnover, getting rid of the offending tiles, and hopefully replacing them with a better balance and one or some of the remaining desirable letters. However, you need to beware the possibility of there being no good tiles remaining, with only awkward letters (such as B, F, Q and V), or perhaps a surfeit of I's or U's, still to come.

There are some types of game where it is important to

maximize your turnover, and there are other types which you need to keep your turnover down. More about this later.

Tile Tracking

You may wish to keep a note beside you of the distribution of tiles in a standard Scrabble set, and cross off individual tiles as they are played. This way, you can see at an instant what tiles are still to come at any point during a game. Tile tracking will enable you to answer immediately, without having to stop and count up, questions such as are there any U's still to come? how many S's are still unplayed? is there a preponderance of vowels still to be played? are there any B's or V's left unplayed? And so on. Tile tracking can also be useful at the end of a game, as it will enable you to see at a glance what letters your opponent is left with. Perhaps he has a valuable S, or the X, or maybe a bonus word. Or maybe he is going to be stuck with the Q and an awkward clump of consonants.

A simple sheet for tile tracking as well as scoring is shown in Figure 71. Some players prefer to arrange the letters differently, grouping all the vowels together, the high-value tiles together, and so on. There are numerous possibilities – Figure 72 shows an alternative layout.

While tile tracking is permitted in tournament Scrabble and is allowed by many Scrabble clubs, it is probably worth checking with your opponent to make sure they don't mind your keeping track of the tiles in this way. There is a school of thought which says it is unfair. After all, you are not allowed to keep track of cards played at bridge – so why should you be able to in Scrabble!

SCRABBLE®

My tiles	Words played	Score	Total	Words played	Score	Total

AAAAAAAAA	GGG	NNNNNN	UUUU
BB	HH	OOOOOOOO	VV
CC	IIIIIIIII	PP	WW
DDDD	J	Q	X
EEEEE	K	RRRRRR	YY
EEEEE	LLLL	SSSS	Z
FF	MM	TTTTT	blank blank

Figure 71: A 2-player score-sheet, for tile tracking

SCRABBLE®

My tiles	Words played	Score	Total	Words played	Score	Total

A A A A A A A A A	D D D D	B B	V V	J
E E E E E	G G G	C C	W W	K
E E E E E	L L L L	F F	Y Y	Q
I I I I I I I I I	N N N N	H H		X
O O O O O O O O	R R R R R	M M		Z
U U U U	T T T T T	P P		S S S S
				blank blank

Figure 72: A 2-player score-sheet, for tile tracking – an alternative layout of letters

Documenting Moves

In Chapter 2, the labelling of the rows and columns of the Scrabble board was referred to. The columns are labelled A to O, going from left to right; and the rows are labelled 1 to 15, going from top to bottom. Any square on the board can be defined precisely by giving its column and row labels – for example, A1, B4, J6, N10 and O9. Earlier in this chapter, use was made of this labelling system. In referring to Figure 66, it was explained that the word EXPORT could be played across, using the P already on the board, for 62 points. A much more concise way of documenting this move, its position and score is to record:

I2a, EXPORT (62)

Note that the letter 'a' stands for 'across'. This says the word EXPORT was played, starting at square I2, going across, and scored 62 points. One of the other moves possible in Figure 66 was the word EXERT. The concise way of documenting this would be:

H8d, EXERT (21)

In this particular move involving EXERT, the word AX was also made. However, it is not necessary to record this separately. This is implicit in 'H8d, EXERT (20)'. Examination of the board and the main word played will reveal the creation of AX, going across from G9. Consequently, any move, involving from one to eight words created, can be summarized in this compact way. Consider the situation shown in Figure 15: ANIMATE was already on the board, and SATIRES was then played parallel to and beneath it, making seven two-letter words at the same time. It is unnecessary to refer to these seven additional words. Merely recording 'B9a, SATIRES (77)' is sufficient to document the entire move. This notation will be used in the remaining chapters.

There is an alternative way of recording moves, which has some currency, especially in the USA. This is to omit the use of an 'a' or 'd', and to define the column or row first, depending on whether the main word played goes down or across. An across word is denoted by referring to the row first (for example, 8A). A down word is denoted by referring to the column first (for example, A8). There is a logic to this. Take the example of a five-letter word played across from 8A: the word would stretch from

8A to 8E, or 8A-E. The '-E' is redundant, and so the position could be recorded as merely 8A. However, this notation requires the reader to stop and think whether a particular word has been played across or down. Use of 'a' and 'd' makes the situation simpler, and saves you having to work out whether the notation implies an across word or a down word.

High-scoring Versus Winning

Over the years, two very distinctive styles of Scrabble game have developed. One style involves playing for high scores; and the other is about playing to win, almost (but not quite) regardless of score.

Playing for high scores can be traced back to the format of the National Scrabble Championship between the years 1971 and 1989, and the copycat format adopted by most club tournaments during that time. The winners of these events were determined by players' total scores over three or four games. It did not matter whether players won or lost their games. All that was important was achieving high scores in the individual games. Much better to lose with 500 points than to win with 350 points. Because of the need to score highly, players became skilled at techniques necessary to achieve scores of 600+ and even 700+. (The author's highest score in such a game stands at 803 points.) The techniques necessary to gain these sorts of very high scores are explained in the succeeding chapter, Playing Well for High Scores.

During the late 1980s, there was pressure from a considerable number of experienced Scrabble players to move away from playing for high scores, and to move back to playing to win. This was more in keeping with the game's early origins, where the game's inventor had obviously intended that winning should be more important than scoring highly. As a result of this pressure, the format of many club tournaments moved towards the playing-to-win style, and the National Scrabble Championship followed suit in 1990. In a tournament of three, four, nine or even 15 games, the winner would be determined by the number of wins achieved. Playing to win, rather than playing for a high score, demands a very different style of play. Techniques and tips for improving your chances of winning are explained in Chapter 6, Playing Well to Win.

5

Playing Well for High Scores

Introduction

This chapter explains concepts, techniques and tips that you will need to be aware of and make use of if you and your opponent want to achieve high scores. What sorts of high scores? The techniques covered in this chapter are those used by experienced Scrabble players to reach scores of 600+, occasionally 700+ and even the odd 800+. Of course, following the advice in this chapter won't guarantee these sorts of scores in all or even most games, but it will lead to higher scores, on average, in the long run. There will be occasions in real games when the advice given in one part of this chapter seems to run counter to that given in another part. You will have to weigh up the relative pros and cons of such situations, and make what you think is the correct decision. Taking into account all the advice offered here, you should net scores between 450-550 on many occasions.

It is important to note that these techniques will only work if both you and your opponent share the same objective of achieving high scores. If one of you is playing for high scores and the other is merely playing to win, not caring whether his final score is 250 or 650, then the chances are that the playing-to-win player will win! Playing for high scores is based on the mutual understanding that both players will make moves that facilitate subsequent high-scoring moves to the advantage of both players. If one player upsets this unvoiced arrangement, then there is no point in continuing to try for high scores.

General Principles

Three overriding principles apply to high-score games.

The first principle is to squeeze every ounce of value out of your tiles. Play them out slowly, except for the bonuses. Try to keep your turnover of tiles low – except for those valuable bonuses. You should be looking to play one or two tiles at a turn, yet scoring well in between your bonus plays. If you have to choose between playing five tiles for 30 points and two tiles for 24 points, it may well be better in the long run to opt for the 24 points. The longer you can make the tiles last, the more chance there is of your final score edging up into the 450 + region! Also, you should create scoring opportunities for yourself by putting the appropriate letters next to the various premium squares.

The second principle is that you will have to make several bonus plays during the course of a game, in order to pick up the extra 50 points each time. You should probably expect to make at least three, if not more, bonuses during a game. Five, six and seven bonuses by a single player in a game are not unknown. This level of bonus plays does not come about by chance. You have to work to get these plays. You need to have the right letters on your rack, you have to be able to spot bonus words, and you need to be able to fit them on the board.

The third principle is that throughout the game the board needs to be kept 'open'. You should always strive to ensure that there are plenty of hooks that you can attach bonus words to, that you make the 3W premium squares accessible, and that you don't make moves which stifle the board's openness for later on in the game.

These principles are expanded in the following sections.

The Opening Move
The first move in the game can have a considerable influence on how the rest of game progresses. It can quite drama-tically influence the final 'shape' of the board. Unless you have been lucky enough to spot a seven-letter word with your first rack of tiles, the first word played should be short, probably two or three letters. Although the first word played can go across in row 8 or down in column H, it will be assumed to go across in row 8 for convenience. Try to position the vowels so that they are above and beneath the 2L squares on rows 7 and 9. This will give you (and your opponent) the opportunity of scoring well from appropriately positioned consonants on these premium squares in the next move or two.

Figure 73 shows two ways of positioning EWE. The first (G8a) is far preferable to the second (F8a), although the scores are exactly the same (12 points).

	A	B	C	D	E	F	G	H	I	J
1	3W			2L				3W		
2		2W				3L				3L
3			2W				2L		2L	
4	2L			2W				2L		
5					2W					
6		3L				3L				3L
7			2L				2L		2L	
8	3W			2L		E	W	E		
9			2L				2L		2L	

	A	B	C	D	E	F	G	H	I	J
1	3W			2L				3W		
2		2W				3L				3L
3			2W				2L		2L	
4	2L			2W				2L		
5					2W					
6		3L				3L				3L
7			2L				2L		2L	
8	3W			2L	E	W	E			
9			2L				2L		2L	

Figure 73: The first move
Above, right! Below, wrong!

If your first play is a word of three or more letters, position it
so that both halves of the board (top and bottom, or left and
right) are accessible. This gives the potential for bonus plays
which make 3W squares accessible. Figure 74 shows that the
correct positioning of EWE (G8a) allows for the possibility of
bonus words reaching columns A and O, thereby opening up
the 3W squares in those columns. As ever, there is no
guarantee that either player will be able to follow on swiftly
with bonus plays. But the board is being set up so that if or
when such bonuses are put down, then the 3W squares in the
extreme columns will be accessible.

	A	B	C	D	E	F	G	H	I	J	K	L	M	N	O
1	3W			2L				3W				2L			3W
2		2W				3L				3L			2W		
3			2W				2L		2L				2W		
4	2L			2W				2L				2W			2L
5					2W						2W				
6		3L				3L			3L					3L	
7	T	R	A	I	N	E	R		W	E	S	T	E	R	N
8	3W			2L			E	W	E			2L			3W
9			2L				2L		2L				2L		
10		3L				3L			3L					3L	
11				2W							2W				
12	2L			2W				2L				2W			2L
13			2W				2L		2L				2W		
14		2W				3L				3L			2W		
15	3W			2L				3W				2L			3W

Figure 74: Bonuses opening up 3W squares

If you have the option of positioning your word further to the
left than to the right, then by all means play it further to the
left, but still trying to ensure that there is a position for a bonus
play to the right, providing access to column O. 'Playing to the
left' is a useful rule of thumb, as it can be only too easy to keep
building words on the right-hand side of the board, leaving the
left-hand side difficult to get to. The more you 'play to the left',
the less chance there is of this happening. Suppose your first
word is FOOT. This could be played at any of E8a, F8a, G8a

and H8a. E8a is a good position because it opens up the two 2W squares at E5 and E11, but it does mean that any bonus played from H7a or H9a will not reach column O. E9a does not open up the two 2W squares, but does allow for bonuses played at I7a and I9a to reach column O. E10a is positioned too far to the right. And E11a is also too far to the right, although the T provides access to the 2W squares at K5 and K11.

Playing Vowels Next to Premium Squares

Where possible, try to play vowels adjacent to premium squares, especially the 3L squares. A strategically placed O will often provide a hefty score from the J, X or the Z, with the likes of JO, OX or ZO being made. Even a medium-value letter like the W can score quite well from a 2L square, as long as it is making words in both directions.

Figure 75 shows the words EWE, YE and OY already on the board. The O is beneath the 3L square at F6. This offers a splendid opportunity for ZO (F6a) to score 68 points. JO in the same position is worth 56 points. To score well from that 3L square doesn't demand that you have the J or Z. For example, HA would score 32 points, as would WE, and so on.

	A	B	C	D	E	F	G	H	I	J	
1	3W			2L				3W			
2		2W				3L				3L	
3			2W				2L		2L		
4	2L			2W				2L			
5					2W						
6		3L				3L				3L	
7			2L			O	Y		2L		
8	3W			2L			E	W	E		
9			2L				2L		2L		

Figure 75: Playing a vowel next to a 3L square

The Need for 50-Point Bonuses

Playing out all seven of your tiles in one go will score you an extra 50 points. If you can do this several times during a game, you may well find yourself with a total of 150, or even 250, bonus points by the end of a game. These bonus points will certainly help to lift your scores into the 500 + region.

Many inexperienced players believe that bonuses just happen – you have either got one or you haven't. Not so! Most bonuses have to be worked for, planned for, striven for! If you have the first turn in a game and find you can make a bonus word with your first seven tiles, even that is not 100% lucky. You will need to spot the appropriate word from your seven tiles. Later in the game, playing bonuses requires more skill and less luck. Even if you make the conscious decision to exchange all seven of your tiles and the seven new ones from the bag make a word, the bonus depends on at least three things. One, having the experience to recognize that all seven tiles need exchanging. Two, your ability to spot the appropriate bonus word from the tiles on your rack, perhaps in combination with one or some tiles already on the board. And three, whether you can play your tiles anywhere on the board. Have you kept the board open? Have you created hook positions that will accommodate your bonus? Have you provided access to premium squares? Many inexperienced players complain that, even though they can see a seven-letter word on their rack, it will not go down anywhere on their board. Bad luck or bad planning?

So, what makes bonuses happen? The following sections explain the factors contributing to their occurrence.

Blanks and S's Suggest Bonuses!
If you manage to pick a blank or an S from the bag, you should begin to feel that you are close to a 50-point bonus. Because a blank can be used to represent any letter of the alphabet, you will find it makes your tiles far more flexible. With a blank on your rack, you should not play it for anything less than a 50-point bonus. This will usually mean a score of 70 + points.

There may be occasions when you can use a blank to score this sort of score, although there is no bonus play involved. For example, you may need to use it along with a Q or a Z in order to reach a 3W square. If you had the letters QUZ on your rack, plus a blank and three other tiles, you might decide to play – if the board allows – A1a, QUIZ, for well over 100 points, using the blank as an I. That is a perfectly legitimate use of the blank. If you are near the end of a game, there may be no more bonus-scoring possibilities, in which case you will have to accept perhaps only 20-40 points for using the blank.

The presence of an S on your rack is also a powerful pointer to an upcoming bonus. Because an S so easily hooks on to the end of words (and to the front of many others), you should retain an S for a bonus play. Although an S is not as powerful as a blank, it is a very valuable tile to have on your rack, but its value can only be realized by playing it well.

Bonuses from the Low-value Letters

The one- and two-point tiles combine far more easily with each other than with the higher value tiles in order to make seven- and eight-letter words. You will find the low-value tiles much easier to manipulate. They occur in so many different but recurring sequences – some of the commoner ones were listed in the previous chapter. The more low-value tiles on your rack, the greater the chance of your finding a seven-letter word from them, or combining them with a letter already on the board to create an eight-letter word.

Of course, this advice has to be absorbed in conjunction with that on rack balancing in a later section. You are less likely to find a bonus word while holding two D's and two N's on your rack than if you are holding one each of D, N, R and T.

When You're Close to a Bonus . . .

How do you know when you are close to achieving a bonus? If you have four, five or six easy-to-use letters, then you may well be near to a bonus play. The following section lists some of these easy-to-use combinations. If you have any of these on your rack, be prepared to play off the other one, two or three tiles, or maybe even exchange them.

In playing off a few tiles like this, though, you should still be striving for a reasonable score. There is little point in playing the letters EIL for 4-5 points. That's a waste of the tiles! If you cannot score 20 + points even on a simple discard like this, be prepared to exchange the tiles. You are bound to get more value from them if they come back to you later. If there are relatively few places on the board to play a bonus, though, you should consider using your discard tiles to make an additional opening, perhaps making a simple hook word somewhere. In this case, a relatively poor score could be justified.

Common Letter Combinations

'Easy-to-use' combinations of letters were referred to in the last section. Although many Scrabble players have an intuitive feel for these, it is probably worth giving some examples here, to ensure you are clear about what makes up such a combination. 60 examples of five-letter combinations follow:

ADEIN	AELRT	DEINT	DESTU	EINRS	GILNU
ADEIR	AELST	DEIRS	EGILN	EINRT	GINOR
ADEIS	AENRS	DEIRT	EGILS	EINST	GINOS
AEILS	AENST	DEIST	EGINR	EIRST	GINOT
AEINS	AERST	DELRS	EGINS	ENORS	GINRS
AEINT	DEILN	EGINT	EGINT	EORST	GINST
AEIRS	DELST	DENOR	EILNS	ERSTU	GNORS
AEIRT	DEILT	DENOS	EILNT	GILNS	GNOST
AEIST	DEINR	DENOT	EINOS	GILNT	ILNOS
AELRS	DEINS	DERST	EINOT	GILNO	INOST

What about promising six-letter combinations? Here are 60 of these:

ADEERS	ADENST	AEGNST	AELRST	DEGINR	EEILST
ADEGNR	ADGINR	AEILRS	AENRRT	DEGINS	EGILNR
ADEINR	AEELRS	AEILST	AENSTT	DEILNS	EGILST
ADEIRS	AEERST	AEINRT	AERRST	DEINRS	EGINRS
ADEIST	AEGILN	AEIRST	AERSTT	DEIRST	EGINST
ADELNS	AEGLNR	AEISTT	AGINRT	DEIRSU	EILNST
ADELST	AEGLNT	AELNST	AINRST	DELORS	EINRST
ADENRS	AEGLRS	AELORS	ANORST	DENRSU	GINOST
ADENRU	AEGNRS	AELOST	DEENRS	DEORST	INORST

Of course, there are many gaps in this short list. Try and come up with another 60 or so combinations of your own.

Rack Balancing

The concept of rack balancing was introduced in the previous chapter. As far as possible, you should strive to keep a balanced rack of vowels and consonants. Ideally, your rack should contain two or three vowels, and four or five consonants. On average, for every four vowels you take from the bag, you will take five consonants. That's roughly an equal split. If you have a rack of letters which has an excess of vowels (four or more), try to play off the excess ones. Similarly with consonants. If you can get rid of these excesses, your vowel-consonant distribution will tend to return to a better balance as you randomly select new tiles from the bag.

This advice needs to be tempered with any special knowledge you may have, given the state of any particular game. For example, if you are close to the end of a game, you may be aware that there are relatively few vowels still to come from the bag. If you have five vowels on your rack, it might be unwise to use them up too quickly. You may well find you encounter problems with excessive consonants in a turn or two's time.

Rack balancing is more subtle than just trying to get a vowel-consonant balance. You should also be striving to minimize duplicate letters. Although two blanks, two S's or two E's will not cause problems, you may find that having two of various other letters leads to difficulties. Duplicates, or even triplicates, need breaking up fairly quickly. Two of a particular letter may not be a problem, but don't overlook the possibility of picking a third or even fourth one from the bag when you select replacement tiles. Two I's will hamper you; a third one from the bag will restrict you even further. Two U's is bad enough, but a third will present real problems. A pair of L's or N's on your rack may well be manageable, but a third L or N will really reduce your scoring opportunities.

There is another aspect to rack balancing in addition to those already explained. Some letters do not 'go well' together. The combination of LNR is often a poor one, but can be eased by the addition of EI. D and T don't always go well together, although an E (for an -ED ending) helps a lot. GLU can be awkward, unless IN is also present.

Rack Balancing: Some Examples

It isn't easy to give specific advice on what to do with a particular set of seven letters. So much depends on the state of the game: how far through is the game? how many tiles are still to come? what score have you already achieved? how many blanks and S's are still to be played? how strong is your opponent? And so on! Nevertheless, it may be instructive to consider some racks of letters you could find yourself holding. The points made here are those which you would need to assess before making your final choice as to what to do.

Two consonants and five vowels – the imbalance will have to be corrected. Three O's – too many duplicates. At least a couple of O's will have to go. You may be tempted to play OLIVE or VOILE. Don't! First of all, the turnover of five tiles is too high; and second, it will leave a pair of O's on your rack. You might want to exchange the IOOOV. A more reasonable exchange would be IOO, retaining EILV on your rack. Although V can be an awkward letter to use, somehow it seems to 'go' with the EIL combination. Retaining EILV, rather than just EL, gives you more control over your next rack. Playing off just two of the O's, leaving EILOV on your rack, suggests the possibility of a vowel excess problem for your next rack. Keeping back EILOV and then picking up at least one vowel will lead to continuing problems. On balance, the preferred move is to exchange the three O's.

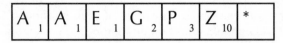

The blank (*) here suggests an early bonus. Three vowels on your rack is reasonable, but one of them is a duplicate A. You ought to consider playing off one of the A's. The G, P and Z don't necessarily go well together. You should be trying to get rid of at least one, maybe two, of them. You might spot the word AGAZE on your rack. But using up five tiles to play it is too great a turnover, unless you manage to score 40 + points with it. Even then, 50 + points would make a five-tile turnover feel more acceptable. If there is an available D somewhere, you might consider AGAZED, but you will still need to score at least 40–50 points from it. How about playing off just three tiles, one of them the Z? What about playing ZEA somewhere? The retention of AGP* could be acceptable, but the G and P still don't go well together. How about ZAG or ZAP somewhere? ZAG will leave you with AEP*. And ZAP will leave you with AEG*, an attractive group of four letters to be left with. Even though this may look attractive, you still need to score well from ZAP, without blocking any hook positions on the board. You will need to pick up at least 30 points from ZAP for it to be worthwhile. Another possibility is to play GAP somewhere, retaining AEZ*, in an attempt to get a bonus play using the Z. It could pay off, but you do need to be aware that an awkward selection of new tiles may thwart your plan! On balance, play ZAP for 30 + points.

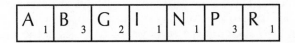

Two vowels and five consonants. The B, G and P don't go well together, but the rack does contain the useful -ING group. No duplicates to worry about. How about playing off just the B? That would leave AGINPR, which is quite a promising group, suggesting possibilities like CARPING, REAPING, PAIRING and so on, following your pickup of one tile. However, the wrong letter picked will take you back to a rack similar to this ABGINPR one that you started with. Better is to play off the B and P – perhaps BAP, BOP or PUB somewhere. If you could pick up 25 points or so for one of these, retention of AGINR is really quite reasonable. One point of caution, though! Try not to get too hung up about retaining the -ING group. Sometimes that can blind you to other possibilities. There are plenty of words with the letters GIN in, but not necessarily as part of an -ING ending. Sometimes even retention of the G doesn't help. But for the time being, AGINR feels a safe yet promising retention.

D₂	G₂	H₄	I₁	K₅	S₁	Y₄

Only one real vowel, the I, although the Y can be used as a vowel or consonant. Call it one-and-a-half vowels and four-and-a-half consonants! The S is promising. Perhaps you can pick up some good scores by judicious use of the H, K and Y. No duplicates, so that's okay. DISHY springs to mind, but has too many considerations against it. The turnover of five tiles is too high; it uses the valuable S; and it leaves the very poor GK on your rack. Is there an E somewhere on the board for HIKE or HIKED? The turnover of three or four tiles counts against these possible plays. Much more attractive is to just play off KY somewhere. Is there a convenient premium square to put either the K or Y on? That should net a reasonable score (30 or so), it keeps the turnover low, and it uses two of the awkward letters. Admittedly, the retention of DGHIS is not brilliant, but you can't have everything! You could always play a word like GHI or HID on your next turn.

Five vowels and only two consonants – another imbalance that needs addressing. Even the two consonants are duplicates. Given that all the letters are single-pointers, there won't be many scoring opportunities here. Playing the all-vowel EUOI might be worthwhile. The turnover of four tiles is rather high, and the retained letters INN could be better. If EUOI only scores a handful of points – say, less than 20 – it would probably be wiser to consider exchanging tiles. You might spot UNION on your rack. Chances are it won't score well, and it will still leave the undesirable EI on your rack. Of course, if there was an N somewhere on the board that you could use, playing UNION would give a rack retention of INE, which is attractive. However, none of these possible moves holds much promise of a reasonable score and they all involve too large a turnover. Go for an exchange of tiles. Keep EN, and change the IINOU.

Use the High-value Letters to Good Effect

In general, the J, K, Q, X and Z should be turned over fairly quickly, but need to earn their keep, points-wise, at the same time. An X or Z played for little more than face value (perhaps ZOO for 14 points) is not really exploiting the potential that such letters offer. These letters should be utilized with premium squares as far as possible. A simple word like ZOO covering a 2W square will net at least 24 points.

On the other hand, retaining these high-value letters too long on your rack will probably reduce the chances of your finding a bonus move.

Going one step further, you should try to be on the lookout for promising combinations of letters using the high-value ones which could generate bonus words. The following combinations and patterns suggest that a high-scoring bonus may not be far away:

J---ERS	-KIER	QUIN-	EX-	-IZED
J---EST	-KIEST	QUITE-	EXC-	-IZES
J---IER	-KING	REQU-	EXP-	-ZIER
J---ING	KN---ED	UNQU-	EXT-	-ZING

The attitude to adopt towards the high-value letters is to make them work for you. Use them quickly and cleanly for a good score. Only hold on to them for two or three turns if you have the early promise of a good bonus word. Remember: none of these letters scores you a single point while it is sitting on your rack!

Don't Hang on to the Medium-value Letters too Long

You should treat the medium-value letters in much the same way as the higher-value ones. Make them work for you, and don't hang on to them for too long. However, you will find the medium-value letters a lot easier to incorporate in bonus words, so do be on the lookout for such bonuses. After all, the H, M and P are really quite easy to use in conjunction with the single-pointers, probably more so than B, F and V. Having one medium-value letter on your rack will not hamstring you. Even two may be manageable, if they go well together. For example, CH, MP and PH 'go well' together. On the other hand, BP, FP and PV are all awkward.

Keeping the Board Open

Compare the board layouts in Figures 76 and 77. Figure 76 shows an 'open' game in its early stages. Early bonus plays (RETAINS and BESTIAL) have provided access to the 3W squares at A8, A15, O1 and O8. The FAIREST bonus covered two 2W squares, thereby quadrupling the face value of the tiles. Notice how the premium squares at F6, F10, I9, J6 and J10 have all been used to good effect. There is plenty of scope still for high-scoring bonus plays. This board has the potential of giving high final scores. Compare this with the board layout in Figure 77. The board has got stuck into a 'ladder sequence' and it will be difficult to fit in several bonuses. There is little chance that the top left-hand corner will be used. Likely positions for bonus words are L6d (you would need an eight-letter word beginning with N!) and H12a (you will need a seven-letter word beginning with any of A, E, I and O). This board suggests little scope for high scores.

	A	B	C	D	E	F	G	H	I	J	K	L	M	N	O
1	3W			2L				3W				2L			3W
2		2W				3L				3L				2W	
3			2W				2L		2L				2W		
4	2L			2W				2L				2W			2L
5					F	A	I	R	E	S	T				
6		3L			A	X			H	E				3L	
7			2L				2L	B	E	S	T	I	A	L	
8	3W			2L		E	V	E				2L			3W
9	R	E	T	A	I	N	S		Z	O			2L		
10		3L			O	Y			H	I				3L	
11					2W						2W				
12	2L			2W				2L				2W			2L
13			2W				2L		2L				2W		
14		2W				3L				3L				2W	
15	3W			2L				3W				2L			3W

Figure 76: An 'open' board

	A	B	C	D	E	F	G	H	I	J	K	L	M	N	O
1	3W			2L				3W				2L			3W
2		2W				3L				3L				2W	
3			2W				2L		2L				2W		
4	2L			2W				2L				2W			2L
5					2W			B	E						
6		3L				3L		T	O	R	N			3L	
7			2L				2L	D	A	Y			2L		
8	3W			2L			P	O	X			2L			3W
9			2L			F	A	H	2L				2L		
10		3L		Q	U	O	D			3L				3L	
11				R	E	S	T				2W				
12	2L			2W				2L				2W			2L
13			2W				2L		2L				2W		
14		2W				3L				3L				2W	
15	3W			2L				3W				2L			3W

Figure 77: A difficult board

Setting up Hook Openings

In order to get your bonus and other high-scoring words down on the board, don't rely on -S plurals and verb forms. Useful as these -S forms are, there are many other hook possibilities, occurring at both ends of words. Most, though certainly not all, of the two-letter words can be extended by the addition of one letter to create a three-letter word.

In this way, you can use up your unwanted tiles – one or two at a time – to leave potential places for bonuses at various positions on the board. In Figure 78, there are various two-letter hook words just crying out to have a third letter added to them.

Figure 78: Two-letter hook words

The two-letter words that could be used for bonus plays, and the three-letter words that could be derived, are summarized below:

AE	AI	DO	HA	ME	UR	ZO
DAE	AIA	ADO	AHA	MEL	BUR	DZO
GAE	AID	UDO	CHA	MEN	CUR	
HAE	AIL		WHA	MES	FUR	
KAE	AIM			MET	GUR	
MAE	AIN			MEU	LUR	
NAE	AIR			MEW	NUR	
SAE	AIS				OUR	
TAE	AIT				PUR	
VAE					SUR	
WAE					URD	
					URE	
					URN	

The other two-letter words which could be extended to become three-letter words, but which could not be used for bonus plays, are BO, ER, GI and JO. Even so, knowledge of the three-letter extensions would be useful for dumping the odd unwanted letter. Consider the square H6. This could take an unwanted A or O for 19 points. Not bad for one tile, especially if it helps to sort out a rack balance problem.

Of course, the concept of hooks also applies to words of more than two letters. Although the two-to-three hooks and seven-to-eight hooks are especially useful in high-score Scrabble, there are many hooks of other lengths. Experienced Scrabble players know most of the three-to-four hooks, many of the four-to-five ones, and some of the five-to-six ones – but these tend to be a lot more frequently used in playing-to-win Scrabble than in high-score Scrabble. More of these longer hooks in the next chapter. *Official Scrabble Lists* methodically documents all the hooks for words of length two to seven letters. Here are some of the more obscure ones that the top Scrabble players keep tucked up their sleeves:

3-to-4	4-to-5	5-to-6	6-to-7	7-to-8
BOA(K)	(N)ACHE	(A)CIDER	(P)ACTION	(P)ALIMONY
COX(Y)	CHIC(A)	(E)CURIE	(N)EDDIES	(A)BANDING
FIG(O)	CORN(U)	(V)ELATE	(H)IDLING	FASCISM(O)
(B)INK	(A)DUST	(B)LANKY	OUTWIT(H)	HOOKIES(T)
NOD(I)	(S)HEEL	(U)PLAID	(F)ULLAGE	MALARIA(N)
RIM(U)	(P)LINK	(E)TRIER	WORMER(Y)	WREATHE(N)

Floating Letters

Floating letters, or 'floaters', are potentially useful for making eight-letter words. Perhaps the seven letters on your rack don't combine to make a word, but maybe they will combine with an eighth letter, already on the board, to make an eight-letter specimen. Perhaps the seven letters on your rack do make a word, but it won't go down anywhere on the board. Or maybe you do have a seven-letter word and it will go down on the board, but there may be the possibility of a higher score using an eighth letter. Try to make plays that provide floating letters,

	A	B	C	D	E	F	G	H	I	J	K	L	M	N	O
1	3W			2L			3W					2L			3W
2		2W				3L			3L					2W	
3			2W				2L		2L				2W		
4	2L			2W				2L				2W			2L
5					2W	**B**					2W				
6		3L				**O**				3L				3L	
7			2L			**T**	2L	**O**	**F**	**T**	**E**	**N**	**E**	**R**	
8	3W			2L		**T**	**H**	**E**	**Y**			2L			3W
9			**C**	**O**	**I**	**L**	2L		2L				2L		
10		3L				**E**				3L				3L	
11					2W	**S**	**E**	**Z**			2W				
12	2L			2W				**I**	**C**	**E**		2W			2L
13			2W				2L	**P**	2L				2W		
14		2W				3L		**P**		3L				2W	
15	3W			2L				**Y**				2L			3W

Figure 79: Floating letters

potentially useful for later moves. If there are floating letters already on the board, try not to block them with your intermediate plays between bonuses. Floating letters are potentially more useful if they are the single-point, easy-to-use letters. A floating E or R holds much greater potential than a floating W, for example. Take a look at Figure 79.

Your rack contains the letters AEINORT. If you know the anagrams of the common seven-letter groupings, you will see you have OTARINE here. There is only one place that this will go down on the board: K9d, for 70 points. However, you may not know OTARINE. If you consider the various floating letters, other plays are possible, some worth more than 70 points. First of all, which are the floating letters? The floaters are:

> the B of BOTTLES;
> the C and O of COIL;
> the first P of ZIPPY, but only as the eighth letter of a
>   potential bonus (unlikely!);
> the second P and Y of ZIPPY;
> the E, N, E and R of OFTENER.

What can be achieved with these floaters? The plays and scores that are available to you are these:

> C2d, ANORETIC (72);
> C6d, REACTION (72);
> D14a, ATROPINE (64);
> F5a, BARITONE (70);
> E5a, OBTAINER (90);
> L3d, INORNATE (68);
> L6d, INORNATE (68);
> N3d, ANTERIOR (62).

OBTAINER is obviously the best move here. Even if you didn't know OBTAINER, you ought to be able to spot everyday words like REACTION, BARITONE and ANTERIOR. Although their scores fall short of that of OBTAINER, it is better to pick up 60-70 points rather than miss a bonus completely!

Providing Access to the 3W Squares

The eight triple-word-score (3W) squares are the most valuable on the board. Try to provide easy access to them. If you
can play a bonus word through a 3W square, it is obviously
advantageous to rake in the extra points. Even if you cannot
play a bonus, the effects of a 3W square on your Q word or Z
word are powerful.

Consider the board position in the top part of Figure 80, with
EWE, ZO (twice), COY and OYE already having been played.
Suppose you have the tiles AEEGLNR on your rack. Perhaps you
spot the word ENLARGE fairly quickly. If you play ENLARGE
from H9a, that also makes the vertical words WE and EN,
scoring a total of 69 points – see the lower part of Figure 80.
Although the final E of ENLARGE falls on the N9 square, it
provides access to the 3W squares at O8 and O15, because
ENLARGE is a hook word. Any of D, N, R and S can be added to
ENLARGE, thereby offering a valuable place for a subsequent
high-scoring move.

	A	B	C	D	E	F	G	H	I	J	K	L	M	N	O
1	3W			2L				3W				2L			3W
2		2W				3L			3L				2W		
3			2W				2L		2L				2W		
4	2L			2W				2L				2W			2L
5					2W						2W				
6		3L			Z	O			3L				3L		
7			2L		C	O	Y		2L				2L		
8	3W			2L			E	W	E			2L			3W
9			2L				2L		2L				2L		
10		3L				3L			3L				3L		

	A	B	C	D	E	F	G	H	I	J	K	L	M	N	O
1	3W			2L				3W				2L			3W
2		2W				3L			3L				2W		
3			2W				2L		2L				2W		
4	2L			2W				2L				2W			2L
5					2W						2W				
6		3L			Z	O			3L				3L		
7			2L		C	O	Y		2L				2L		
8	3W			2L			E	W	E			2L			3W
9			2L				2L	E	N	L	A	R	G	E	
10		3L				3L			3L				3L		

Figure 80: What to do with AEEGLNR?

Setting up 'Nine-timers'

Take another look at the board in the top part of Figure 80. Instead of playing H9a, ENLARGE (69), there are better, although lower-scoring, moves possible. ENLARGE at either I7a or I9a will score 63 points. These are shown in Figure 81. But you will probably ask: why should I sacrifice 6 points to do this? The answer lies in the positioning of the final E, on O7 or O9. In either of these positions, it now becomes possible to play seven letters around that floating E, in order to make an eight-letter word straddling two 3W squares. With the final E of ENLARGE on O7, the 3W squares at O1 and O8 are both available for a suitable eight-letter word. Similarly, with the final E of ENLARGE on O9, the 3W squares at O8 and O15 are open for the right word! There is hardly anything to choose between these two possibilities. The floating E on O7 suggests eight-letter words ending with -ED, -ER and -ES. And the floating E on O9 suggests eight-letter words beginning BE-, DE- and RE-. A word eventually played across two 3W squares is affectionately known as a 'nine-timer'. A nine-timer using only one-point letters will score 122 or 131 points, depending on whether the 2W square in it has been covered on a previous turn. If the nine-timer uses any medium-value or high-value letters, then the score for the word will be that much higher.

	A	B	C	D	E	F	G	H	I	J	K	L	M	N	O
1	3W			2L				3W				2L			3W
2		2W				3L				3L				2W	
3			2W				2L		2L				2W		
4	2L			2W				2L				2W			2L
5					2W						2W				
6		3L			Z	O				3L				3L	
7			2L		C	O	Y		E	N	L	A	R	G	E
8	3W			2L			E	W	E			2L			3W
9			2L				2L		2L				2L		

	A	B	C	D	E	F	G	H	I	J	K	L	M	N	O
1	3W			2L				3W				2L			3W
2		2W				3L				3L				2W	
3			2W				2L		2L				2W		
4	2L			2W				2L				2W			2L
5					2W						2W				
6		3L			Z	O				3L				3L	
7			2L		C	O	Y		2L				2L		
8	3W			2L			E	W	E			2L			3W
9			2L				2L		E	N	L	A	R	G	E
10		3L				3L				3L				3L	

Figure 81: Opening up nine-timers

You might feel that the occurrence of such a nine-timer is likely to be extremely rare. Firstly, it requires a suitably easy letter to use to be positioned as a floater between two 3W squares; secondly, it requires that neither player makes use of the position for a lesser move; and thirdly, it requires that either of the players has just the right letters to fill the gap between the two beckoning red squares. However, interposing a letter between two 3W squares in this way, to create a nine-timer possibility, is a frequent artifice in games where players are seeking high scores. By mutual but unvoiced agreement, players will leave such positions open until one or other of them manages to get the nine-timer. Many high-score tournament games have multiple numbers of nine-timer set-ups available on the board at any one time.

Occasionally, one or other player will need to use a nine-timer opening in order to play a bonus word which only covers one of the two red squares. While that may be unfortunate, there is usually little reason to withhold playing such a move. After all, an *actual* score of 80+ points is preferable to a *possible* score of 130+ points. If you need to use a nine-timer position to cover just one of the 3W squares, you ought to be prepared to open up another such nine-timer set-up somewhere else on the board in the next move or two, assuming there isn't another such set-up already available.

At high-score Scrabble tournaments, playing of nine-timers is de rigueur. The author recalls two particularly high-scoring nine-timers he played at Scrabble tournaments. The first involved A1d, CONQUERS (311); and the second was A15a, DRUXIEST (266). Note that the scores here are those achieved on the turns in question – they are not the final game scores!

Avoid Inadvertent Blocking Moves

When you make a move, do consider whether you are inadvertently blocking some particularly useful part of the board. Does your play negate the value of a hook? Does it use one or more floating letters, making them unavailable for a later bonus play? Does it deny access to a 3W square? Or merely make it more difficult? Have you messed up a nine-timer position? Have you blocked the only accessible U on the board, with the other

U's already inaccessible and the Q still to come? Are you allowing the board to develop the sort of 'ladder' arrangement shown in Figure 77? Have you played your 25-point move, only to jeopardize a superb position for a bonus later on? With a nine-timer set-up on the board, it really isn't worth taking just one of the accessible red squares for anything less than a bonus play. Telling yourself that 39 points or 48 points is worth having is a misjudgement. If you cannot score at least 75 + from one of the 3W squares in a nine-timer set-up, then do something else! Leave the nine-timer position available for later use.

There is a difference between inadvertently making a blocking move and a more considered effort to block some part of the board. There are several good reasons why you may wish to play a move which could be considered a blocking one. It may be the only place to put down your bonus play. You might be able to play the Q or Z for a welcome 50 + points. There may be so many hooks on the board and premium squares available that blocking one or a few of them does not matter. It may be so near to the end of the game that it doesn't matter about leaving these positions open any longer. If you can justify to yourself why you should play a particular blocking move, bearing in mind that you are aiming for the highest score possible in a game, then go ahead and do it.

Reading Your Opponent's Plays
You will need to consider whether your opponent has the same objective as you – namely, to achieve a particularly high score.

Is he making moves with a low turnover of tiles? If so, fine. But if he keeps playing longer words, perhaps four and five letters, then you will find that he will be racing through the tiles far more quickly than you, perhaps getting 55-60 of them, compared with your 40-45.

Is he making good use of the premium squares, perhaps picking up 25-30 points for two letters? Is he creating new hook positions? Or is he using them for mediocre scores?

Consider the possibilities following on from each of your opponent's moves. Do they offer any hook possibilities – perhaps difficult ones that you may not know or may not spot immediately, and that your opponent intends to keep for himself? Some words have some rather unexpected hooks – for example PAYS(D) and QUAY(D).

Does your opponent keep blocking floating letters, intentionally or otherwise? It can be very easy to block off three or four floating letters by playing a word parallel to them , but denying them to you for your forthcoming eight-letter word. Consider the board layout shown earlier in Figure 79. The play of I14d, OU (11) effectively blocks the final -PY of ZIPPY. The play of C10a, HI (14) blocks the floating C and O of COIL. Both of these could be considered blocking plays where similar scores could have been achieved elsewhere. However, consider the floating ENER of OFTENER. A move such as L8a, OLEA (22) manages to block all the floaters, yet achieve a meagre 22 points. Not particularly justifiable. Alternatively, a move like K8a, XYLEM (85) is entirely justifiable, even if the effect is still to block the floaters. Blocking floaters for a good score may be acceptable; blocking them for a paltry score is not!

Your opponent may also be the type of player who will quite happily – but unfortunately – take a valuable nine-timer position for 50 points or less. If he is, you will just have to resign yourself to the fact that neither of you is likely to end up with a stunning total score.

If you get the opportunity, consider these issues before you start providing easy access to 3W squares, setting up nine-timer positions, and playing useful hooks.

Does your opponent seem to be near to a bonus? Is he playing just one or two letters for a few points, obviously trying to discard unwanted tiles from his rack, in anticipation of an early bonus? What openings are available for bonuses on the board? If there is only one, is your opponent likely to get to it before you do? If so, perhaps you should create additional openings, so that both you and your opponent will get your bonus plays down.

Is your opponent exchanging tiles? How many tiles? Exchanging one or two tiles suggests he is close to a bonus, and is 'fishing' for the right tile or two get a bonus. Exchanging three or more tiles suggests he has problems – perhaps awkward letters, perhaps the Q, maybe too many vowels, or no vowels at all. All the while your opponent is struggling like this, the less chance there is of him taking or obstructing the various hooks, floating letters and available premium squares.

All these considerations may give you some insight into your opponent's capabilities, and how he is likely to respond to your moves. Equally, ask yourself how your moves appear to an accomplished opponent. Are you doing the wrong things? There is often a temptation to play a poor strategic move, telling yourself that you were unable to do anything else. The chances are there was a better strategic move, even if it was only to exchange tiles.

End-game Play

The obvious point to remember is that the player who goes out first has added to his score the face value of the unplayed tiles on the opponent's rack. Conversely, the opponent's score is reduced by the face value of those tiles. This can be quite an important consideration.

How should you adjust your play towards the end of a game? What factors are important?

First of all, you need to be quite clear whether it is necessary for you to win the game or to score as many points as possible! It was pointed out earlier that for many years the National Scrabble Championship was decided merely on high scores, with absolutely no importance being attached to winning. However, all players like to win, and there can often be a temptation to win with 500 points, rather than to lose with 520 points. So, be clear about this!

The end of a game is approaching. There are still more than seven tiles in the pool of unplayed ones. Is it worth one last exchange of tiles, in order to get rid of your awkward letters? Suppose there are nine tiles remaining in the bag, and you are holding ABEHPQV. Are there any floating U's on the board? Probably not. You could exchange one or two tiles, if you wished. Perhaps it would be worth returning the Q and V. Before exchanging any tiles, though, you should consider what the unplayed tiles are – those in the bag and on the opponent's rack. Is there any way you are going to be able to play the Q and V, the most awkward of this bunch? If you can play QAT

Playing Well for High Scores

or QI or QOPH, then by all means do, regardless of whether you cover any premium squares. If you are unable to play these letters, and there is no likelihood of a Q word coming up, then do exchange them. But . . . There may still be difficult letters to come – perhaps a B, F and W! Returning tiles to the pool at this late stage can be risky. One, you are missing a scoring opportunity; two, your opponent may be able to put them to good use; and, three, you may get replacement tiles that are almost as bad as those returned. There can be occasions when you should just accept you are going to get caught with the Q or V or whatever, and to play on regardless.

If you are playing for high scores only, then getting caught with the Q will reduce your final score by 10. If there is any element of playing-to-win, then getting caught with the Q will not only reduce your score by 10 points, it will increase the opponent's score by 10 points. A 20-point lead on your part could suddenly disappear!

Once there are no tiles left in the bag, you should be able to work out what your opponent is holding. If you have been tile-tracking, this is simple. If you haven't been tracking, you will have to work out what is still unplayed, given that you know the distribution of tiles. Start off by counting the high-value letters, then the medium-value ones, and finally the single-pointers. Don't forget to count the blanks, but you will probably know immediately whether there are any of these still to be played.

Having determined your opponent's letters, think about what he is likely to do with them. Has he got a seven-letter word? Will it go down anywhere on the board? Is there any possibility of an eight-letter bonus through a floating letter? If he has one or more bonus plays possible, you should assume he will see them and that he will go out on his next turn, catching you with whatever tiles are then on your rack. Accordingly, you should try to stop him going out. Prolonging the game will enable you to rake in more points, increasing your score as much as you are able to. If he has more than one option, can you make a play which will block these options? You will need to block them all. If the options are in very different parts of the board, you will probably find you are unable to block all of them. Block the ones that enable you to score the most from your blocking move. If your opponent has only one option for his bonus, then block it with as high-scoring a move as you can.

If your opponent doesn't have any bonus plays available, then you should strive to go out before he does. Remember, you will get the face-value points of the tiles on his rack. Plan your final moves. Can you go out in two turns? Can your opponent go out in two turns?

If he blocks one of your possible plays, do you have an alternative? Try to play off your higher-scoring tiles first. It is usually better to play your M and P, and get caught with two A's, rather than the other way round. But you should check the scores. If playing off your two A's and getting caught with M and P scores more points than vice versa, then go for the play which maximizes your final score.

Even though both players have seven or less tiles on their racks, it can be possible to set up plays that you can build on, thereby enabling you to score more. This can quite often be the case if you have medium- or high-value tiles, some reasonable vowels, and maybe an S.

Of course, if your opponent has an unplayable Q – or perhaps a V – you can take as many moves as you like to go out, slowly building up your total score.

Sample High-scoring Games
Putting all the advice in the preceding sections together can pose a daunting task. In a real game, you will not necessarily get the opportunity of doing or even considering all the points discussed here. In practice, your nine-timer set-ups may not come off. Your tile exchanges may not bring you the tiles you are seeking. Your opponent may have what seems to be an unusual amount of luck in getting blank tiles and bonus moves.

However, what might a high-scoring game look like where most of these factors were relevant at some point during the game? Two sample high-scoring games are shown here. Figure 82 shows the final board layout of a high-scoring game that you might have played; and Figure 83 is a record of the individual moves and scores achieved by you and your opponent during the game. Figures 84 and 85 represent a second high-scoring game.

Various comments concerning each of the moves are also given. What better plays were missed? What other considerations should have been made? Should you have scored better? Should you have exchanged more often? Less often? What about your opponent's moves? What did he miss? Should he have won? If not, how much closer could he have got to your score?

Sample High-scoring Game (No. 1)

	A	B	C	D	E	F	G	H	I	J	K	L	M	N	O
1	E	A		2L				3W				M	O	P	S
2	X	I				3L			3L			O		2W	
3	A		2W				2L		V		J	O	B		
4	M	I		2W				Q	I		A	T	E		2L
5		N		R	A	N	T	I	N	G	S		D		
6		L				Y	O			U	P			3L	
7	T	A	B	L	I	E	R		K	Y	E		2L		
8	3W	N	O	2L	N		E	W	E		2L				O
9		D	I		D		2L		F	A	T		2L		U
10		E	L		U	3L			S	H	E	R	I	A	T
11	A	R	E		C						W	E			V
12	Z		R	2W	T		2L				F	A			O
13	O		S			2L		2L					H	I	T*
14	I	2W				3L				3L				2W	E
15	C			2L			G	R	U	N	T*	L	E	D

Figure 82: The board in a sample high-scoring game (No. 1)

You

Tiles	Move	Score	Total
AEEERSW	G8a, EWE	12	12
AEHIRST	I10a, SHERIAT	91	103
GIIIUV*	exchange GIIUV	0	103
DEOOTUV*	O8d, OUTVOTED (2nd T = blank)	158	261
AAFGINT	L12a, FA	22	283
AGINNRT	D5a, RANTING	76	359
AEKORXY	I7a, KY	30	389
AELMORX	A1d, EXAM	55	444
AAIILOR	B1d, AI	24	468
ACILORZ	A11d, AZOIC	80	548
BDEILRV	M3d, BED	9	587
EGILORV	I3d, VIN	10	597
EGILORS	C7d, BOILERS	31	628
		-2	626

Your Opponent

Tiles	Move	Score	Total
AAEFRTT	I9a, FAT	19	19
AEEIRTW	K11a, WE	24	43
ABEILRT	A7a, TABLIER	66	109
EHINORY	F6a, YO	29	138
EHIILNR	M13a, HIT	20	158
EIILNQR	H4a, QI	44	202
DEILNNR	B4d, INLANDER	63	265
AENPSUU	J6a, UP	14	279
AEJNSTU	K3d, JASPE	56	335
GMNOOTU	L1d, MOOT	31	366
EGLNRU*	H15a, GRUNTLED (T = blank)	77	443
CDNOPSU	L1a, MOPS	24	467
CDNTU	E7d, INDUCT	18	485
		2	487

Figure 83: The racks and moves in a sample high-scoring game (No. 1)

Comments on High-scoring Game 1

your moves   **your opponent's moves**

AEEERSW: Three E's here, and a not so useful W. Play EWE, positioning it so that 2L squares are above and below the E's, and bonus plays starting or finishing next to the E's will reach to columns A and O.

> **AAEFRTT:** Duplicate A's and T's, and an unwanted F. FAT takes care of all these problems, with the F falling on a 2L square in words going in two directions. Note that the A is conveniently placed above a 3L square.

AEHIRST: The anagrams here are HASTIER and the less obvious SHERIAT. There are various places for both words, but the play of SHERIAT is the best. It uses the 3L square at J11 to good effect, and opens up a nine-timer possibility in column O.

> **AEEIRTW:** Play the duplicate E and the medium-value W. WE gets both horizontal and vertical words across a 2W square. Note that TEW takes an S at either end, providing a useful hook for a bonus from E12 and making the 3W square at O8 accessible.

GIIIUV*: Dreadful letters, apart from the blank. Change the obvious six.

> **ABEILRT:** Various anagrams here – LIBRATE, TABLIER and TRIABLE. These could be played from A7a and A9a. TABLIER is preferable to the others as it gets the B on a 2L square, and has a floating T in column A, which is marginally better than a floating L. Note that LIBERATE could also be played, from G1d, also opening up a nine-timer possibility.

DEOOUV*: While this doesn't look a particularly good selection of letters, the floating T of SHERIAT transforms this into OUT-DROVE, OUTMOVED and OUTVOTED. Go for OUTVOTED, keeping the V away from rows 12-15.

> **EHINORY:** This has the makings of a bonus. EINOR is a useful five-letter group, and an H is not a difficult letter to use. YO makes good use of the 3L square at F6.

AAFGINT: A duplicate A, and a not very useful F. Although FA kills off the TEW(S) hook, it opens up the possibility of REFS and REFT.

your moves   **your opponent's moves**

> **EHIILNR:** Still the makings of a bonus are there. HIT kills off the REF hook, but opens up the possibility of AHA and AHS.

AGINNRT: The obvious anagram here is RANTING. You could play it from D5a or G5a. Using the T of TABLIER, you could play TRANTING from A3d or A7d. But TRANTING kills off the nine-timer through the floating T of TABLIER. So, go for RANTING. Playing RANTING at D5a leaves a useful hook position – for an S – at K5.

> **EIILNQR:** Once upon a time, this would have required an exchange of tiles, but not so any longer. Playing off QI still leaves EILNR, a well-balanced rack suggesting a bonus to come. The Q has scored well from the 2L square at H4, making QI in both directions.

AEKORXY: You could play KO from B6a, but this would destroy the nine-timer possibility in column A. Take a reasonable score for the K or X on this move, and then use the other high-value letter on the next move. Playing KY at I7a scores 6 points less than KO, but does leave the nine-timer set-up intact.

> **DEILNNR:** No seven-letter anagrams here, but the floating A of TABLIER allows INLANDER to be played. No other bonuses are possible, so the nine-timer opening in column A had to be messed up.

AELMORX: Was there a four-letter word ending in X that could have been played from A1d? Apart from EXAM, there is also AXEL and MOXA, but EXAM scores additional points.

> **AENPSUU:** Playing UP from J6 creates a hook position for the S at L6. It also leaves AENSU on the rack. The S could be useful for the AH(S) and INLANDER(S) hooks; and EUN could be useful for an eight-letter word at H15a, with the pattern UN----ED.

AAIILOR: Too many vowels. Playing off AI somewhere leaves AILOR, suggestive of an -IAL ending perhaps. AI at B1d scores well off the X of EXAM.

> **AEJNSTU:** A floating I would give JAUNTIES, but there isn't one. Playing off JA somewhere would still leave the possibility of

UN----ED at H15a. But the RANTING hook, for an S, suggests both JASP and JASPE, from K3d. While it might be helpful to retain the E, playing it brings in another 12 points. Go for JASPE in preference to JASP. Although using the S has to be considered carefully, the move does net a very valuable 56 points.

ACILORZ: Various Z words are on this rack – AZOIC, COLZA, COZ, CZAR, ZILA, ZOA, ZOIC and ZORIL. COZ at N6d scores 31 points; ZOA at L2d is worth 37 points; and JIZ at K3a scores 38 points. But far and away the best play is AZOIC from A11d, pulling in 80 points, better than many bonuses.

> **GMNOOTU:** Not much promise of a bonus here. MOOT or TOOM, both from L1d, would score 31 points. A floating M on row 1 might be more difficult to use than a floating T, but the M in a nine-timer would pick up 18 points more than a floating T. GNU isn't that bad a set of letters to retain.

BDEILRV: Five reasonable tiles here, spoiled by the B and V. BEDIM at H1a is possible, but would leave the very unbalanced LRV, as well as blocking the nine-timer position on the top row. BED at M3d scores a very healthy 39 points. Pity you didn't have a second E for BELIVE, which would have scored 57 points. The retention of ILRV isn't great, but could be improved by the pickup of an A or E.

> **EGLNRU*:** The blank tile suggests a bonus is close at hand. The seven tiles can be anagrammed to give BUNGLER, GRUNTLE, LOUNGER and PLUNGER, There isn't an eight-letter word through the floating M, though. The best play seems to be to use the blank as a T and to use the floating D of OUTVOTED, making GRUNTLED.

EGILORV: There are now only two tiles in the bag, plus the seven on the opponent's rack. These nine are CDNOPSSTU. With only two vowels there, any play will need to use the vowels carefully. Is there a nine-timer possibility through the floating M? Anything ending in -MING? What about something beginning OVERM-? What about words ending in -MOUS? There's ENORMOUS and SPERMOUS, but you have too few of the right letters. What about a word ending in -MIER? GLOOMIER fits the bill, and the rack is only a single letter away from this! Can the V be played off by itself, in the hope of picking up the solitary O left? There's just one place for the V, turning IN into VIN at I3d.

your moves   **your opponent's moves**

CDNOPSU: Almost COMPOUNDS through the floating M! But not quite. The eight letters that cannot be seen are EGILORST. Can any seven of those plus the floating M make an eight-letter word? Probably not, but it might be risky to leave the M floating. MOUP is possible, but uses both vowels. While there are three vowels unseen, there is a fair likelihood that the one remaining tile in the bag will not be a vowel. Playing MOPS destroys the nine-timer opening and keeps a vowel back, just in case.

EGILORS: The anagram is GLORIES, but it will not go down anywhere! The opponent has CDNTU, and has two places to go out on the next turn – from E7d and A14a. The only way to block both of these is to play a word of at least five letters from A13a, ensuring that the fifth letter is not an S. ORGIES is one possibility. But that is only worth 14 points. That would block either play of INDUCT by the opponent, still leaving LO on your rack. But the scoring opportunities for LO are minimal. Much better is to grab as many points as possible on this turn, and allow the opponent to go out on his next turn. N1d, PIE, 23 would leave 6 points unplayed on the rack; B8a, DOGIES, 16 would leave 2 points on the rack; D4d, GRILLS, 16 leaves 3 points. But best of all is C7d, BOILERS, 31. This is an excellent play, making four horizontal words in the process. This leaves the single G, worth 2 points, unplayed. Assuming the opponent will go out, this is still a net score of 29 points for this move.

CDNTU: The obvious play is to go out with INDUCT.

Sample High-scoring Game (No. 2)

Figure 84: The board in a sample high-scoring game (No. 2)

You			
Tiles	**Move**	**Score**	**Total**
DEIOPTW	G8a, POW	16	16
DEFILTU	H9a, FEU	11	27
DEEILST	K8a, EE	3	30
ADEILST	H1a, TALIPEDS	149	179
OOOSSS*	(exchange OOSS)	0	179
CNNORS*	M6d, CONNERS (E = blank)	63	242
EEINTVX	N9d, EX	51	293
EIINRTV	O3d, VITRINE	86	379
AAIIKOU	L10d, KAI	33	412
AAIOOSU	(exchange AZOIC)	0	412
BGIRSUY	B14a, RUGBY	51	463
ADGINOS	D12a, OD	17	480
AGINORS	C6d, SOARING	65	545
T*		-1	544

Your Opponent			
Tiles	**Move**	**Score**	**Total**
AADEEHR	I7d, AWE	8	8
ADEEHRV	K3d, HAVERED	86	94
DEGLOPW	L1d PLOW	39	133
ADEGIOY	M3d, YE	34	167
ADGHIIO	J6d, HI	29	196
ADEFGIO	F10a, OAF	17	213
DEGIIMN	G6d, IMP	10	223
DEGILNU	E5d, INDULGE	94	317
EIJLNOZ	G5a, JIZ	34	351
AELMNOT	F13a, OMENTAL	71	422
ABCEQTU	F2a, QUA	34	456
BCEORTT	K12d, BATE	11	467
ACEORST	D1d, COASTER	83	550
		1	551

Figure 85: The racks and moves in a sample high-scoring game (No. 2)

Comments on High-scoring Game 2

your moves   **your opponent's moves**

DEIOPTW: D, P and W don't go well together. At least two of them need playing off, to ensure that the retained letters begin to have some bonus potential. POW provides the central three-letter word to get started, ensuring that bonus plays could reach columns A and O.

> **AADEEHR:** A floating G would give HEADGEAR. What about the floating W for HEADWEAR – is that a word? Perhaps the best thing to do is play the duplicate AE somewhere. AWE provides access to rows 1 and 15 for a suitably placed bonus. Note that the retained D can be hooked on at the end of AWE.

DEFILTU: Ought to play the FU somewhere. Could do J5d,EFT,16, with EFT providing a hook for the retained D and L. But the rack retention of DILU doesn't look too good. Go for FEU, providing a hook for the retained D. The retained letters, DEILT, look quite promising.

> **ADEEHRV:** HAVERED is the obvious word to see on this rack. Could play it from J1d for 71 points – and open up a nine-timer position – or K3d for 86 points. Difficult choice to make. On balance, go for the extra 15 points, given that it doesn't actually block any subsequent nine-timer openings.

DEEILST: Although these letters look good, there is no seven-letter word here. The floating A and V of HAVERED are just one column too far over for LEADIEST and DEVILETS. Shame! Play off a single E, going for a bonus next time. Could do K7a,RE,2 or K8a,EE,3. Go for the EE play, since the retained L will hook on to EE. The opponent is less likely to add anything to EE than RE.

> **DEGLOPW:** Steer clear of GLOWED and PLOWED. They use too many tiles. AWE, already on the board, is a hook for WAWE, but that isn't much use at the moment. Go for GLOW or PLOW at L1d to open up a nine-timer, and in order to play off two of G, P and W. There is little to choose between GLOW and PLOW, so go for the most points.

ADEILST: DETAILS and DILATES are the obvious words on the rack. Could do M6d,DILATES,63 or the much better M3d,DETAILS,90. But is there a nine-timer through the P on

the top row? Is there an anagram of ADEILPST? It may help to
determine the anagrams of ADEILPT, and then see if any take an
S plural. PLAITED doesn't take an S, but TALIPED does! And the P
is in just the right place for TALIPEDS to cover both the 3W
squares.

> **ADEGIOY:** Lots of possibilities here from M3d. Among them
> are: AE,22; EA,22; DAY,34; DEY,34; GAY,34; GEY,34; YE,34; YEA,
> 36; and YEAD,40. Although YEAD scores the best, it doesn't
> seem to be worth playing the AD for the extra 6 points. Play YE
> for 34. The D may be useful for the AWE hook position later.

OOOSSS*: An embarrassment of riches! Playing off O's and S's
individually will not bring in a high final score. To get the best
value from these letters, exchange OOSS, retaining OS*. After
all, there is a 50% chance that the S's will come back later.

> **ADGHIIO:** D, G and H don't go well together. Also, there are too
> many vowels here, and duplicate I's. Could play off something
> like AGIO, GIO, HI and HOI somewhere. Note that HOY provides
> hooks for both AHOY and HOYA. I2a,HI,16 uses up the HI.
> J6a,HE,13 still leaves four vowels on the rack. But J6d,HI,29
> scores well, leaving only three vowels on the rack. Take the 29
> points.

CNNORS*: A four-consonant pick-up. CONNERS is the only
word which springs to mind. Possibilities like ENSCORN and
UNSCORN occur, but neither exists. It's a shame that CONNERS
cannot be played along row 2 somewhere. There's nothing from
the S at O1 either. M6d,CONNERS,63 seems to be the only play
possible. Pity it doesn't even cover a 2W square. Still, at least
it's opened up the bottom part of the board somewhat.

> **ADEFGIO:** A floating L would give FOLIAGED. No such luck,
> though. The OF hook – for OFF and OFT – could be used. That
> would help to get the board developing over to the left-hand
> side. It isn't worth retaining the F. The chances of a bonus word
> ending in F are low. Could play F10a,GIF,20 but that's a bit
> blocky, because there are no front-end hooks for GIF. Much
> more useful is F10a,OAF,17 – providing a hook for G and L.
> With the G already on the rack, that could be very helpful. Play
> OAF, retaining DEGI. That has some bonus potential.

your moves   **your opponent's moves**

EEINTVX: Shame there isn't VIXENET, a small vixen! Best bet is to take the score offered by N9d,EX,51. The retention of EINTV isn't too bad. Normally, V isn't a good letter to retain, but it goes well enough with EINT.

> **DEGIIMN:** What a shame about DEMISING through the floating S. There's not quite enough room to get it down. Play off the duplicate I somewhere, and maybe the M as well. Could do I2a,MI,14 but that makes the top left-hand corner of the board more difficult to use. At the moment, the T takes any of A, E, I and O. AM, from I2d, will only take an I or a P. E11a,MI,10 blocks the floating S at M12 and the OAF hook. Avoid that. Much better is G6d,IMP,10. This provides a hook for any of G (left on the rack!), J, L, P, S and W. This opens up the top left-hand corner, which seems to be struggling to get opened up.

EIINRTV: The standard anagrams are INVITER and VITRINE. There isn't an eight-letter word through the floating S. Options are: C2a,INVITER,66 (this doesn't even cover a 2W square); B2a,VITRINE,76 (this uses a 2W square, but negates the possibility of a nine-timer in column A); A11a,INVITER,74 (opens up a nine-timer); and A11a,VITRINE,74 (which also opens up a nine-timer). There are no usable hooks for IMP and OAF. O3d,VITRINE,86 scores best, uses up a 3W square, and in no way blocks IMP, OAF and the floating S.

> **DEGILNU:** ELUDING and INDULGE are the obvious anagrams. There's no DUELING – that needs two L's. Options are: F12a,INDULGES,74; A5a,ELUDING,77 (which opens up a nine-timer); E9d,ELUDING,75 (also opens a nine-timer); and E5d,INDULGE,94 (covering two 2W squares). Although it's normally wise to open up nine-timer positions, the use of the double-double position is too good to turn down. This doesn't block off any nine-timer set-up plays for later on.

AAIIKOU: Six vowels – ugh! Perhaps an exchange is called for. There are still two S's and a blank to come. But L10d,KAI,33 scores well, and provides plenty of hook possibilities – D, E, F, L, M, N and S. The retention of four vowels is dreadful, but perhaps leave the exchange until the next turn.

> **EIJLNOZ:** Two big ones together! Words on the rack include JIZ, JO, JOLE, LOZEN, ZO and ZONE. Possible plays are: K11a,JAR,20

(leaving the interesting EILNOZ on the rack); B6a,ZEIN,33; G5a,JIZ,34; F2d,ZEIN,35; and F2a,ZEIN,37. Best bet is to use both the J and Z, and move towards a bonus with a good rack retention. Play JIZ, leaving ELNO on the rack.

AAIOOSU: Too many vowels! The time to exchange has finally arrived. Keep the S, obviously. And keep at least one vowel. The Q is still to come, as well as the second blank. Should the U be kept, just in case the Q is picked? Or is that really necessary, given the existence of QI? If the U is kept, then at least one other vowel should be held back, to follow any QU combination. Retain the ISU, and exchange AAOO.

AELMNOT: The anagrams here are LOMENTA (a plural), OMENTAL (an adjective) and TELAMON (a noun with an -ES plural). A floating F would give MATFELON, a floating H would give METHANOL, and a floating S would give SALMONET. But none of these floaters exists. Possible plays are: C2a,TELAMON,65; F13a,TELAMON,69; F13a,OMENTAL,71; and B2a,LOMENTA,74. These all score closely enough to give choice on playing the one which is best for the board. B2a,LOMENTA denies any nine-timer possibility between A1 and A8. F13a,OMENTAL provides good scoring opportunities for later moves: (a) a word through the E at H13 to the 3W square at H15, and (b) a word through the 3L square at F14, perhaps reaching the 2W square at B14. Go for F13a,OMENTAL – it's only 3 points short of the maximum.

BGIRSUY: Possibilities are: A12a,BRIGS,32 (this opens up a nine-timer position, but uses the S); and B14a,RUGBY,51 (leaving the S). The latter is better, as it provides for scoring possibilities off the 3W squares at A15 and H15. Note that an S is retained on the rack, in readiness for the OYS possibility.

ABCEQTU: QUA and QAT are on the rack. Could do F2a,QUA,34 (leaving BCET), or C13d,QUA,24 (leaving BCETU), or K12d,QAT,24 (too useful for an S hook along row 15, given that neither the S nor the blank is on the rack already). Go for F2a,QUA,34.

ADGINOS: GANOIDS is the only word here, but it won't go down anywhere. There isn't an eight-letter word through the floating R and U of RUGBY. GANOIDS plus an R makes ROADINGS, but

your moves   **your opponent's moves**

that doesn't fit in. Keep the S for the OYS possibility. And hold back the ING. Bear in mind that there is still an S and a blank to come. Leave the floating R of RUGBY, but create a new hook possibility. D12a,OD provides a hook for the retained G, N and S.

> **BCEORTT:** Perhaps keep the E for the OYE possibility. Could do A15a,BET,19, which brings the score to only 5 points behind the other player. How about going for broke, though, and opening up another nine-timer position? K12d,BATE,11 does just that, leaving the reasonable CORT on the rack.

AGINORS: Four 'standard' anagrams here: IGNAROS, ORIGANS, SIGNORA and SOARING. Three of these can be played from C6d. What about the floating E on the bottom row, though? None of IGNAROES, ORGANISE and ORIGANES will fit in. And there's nothing through the floating R of RUGBY, either. Go for the highest-scoring move, with the G on C12.

> **ACEORST:** COASTER and COATERS are the only words that can be made from these seven letters. Both of them almost go down in column B. B4d,COASTER suffers from RI not being a word; and B4d,COATERS falls foul of RR not being a word. The floating E on row 15 looks inviting. But the only word formable from ACEORST and the floating E is CREASOTE, and that won't fit. The only other bonus possibility is to fit something into column D, between SOARING and INDULGES. Knowing that SEN and ORD are both acceptable three-letter words allows COAST-ER to be slotted in neatly, for a very rewarding 83 points. The other player is left with a T and a blank. Victory snatched from the jaws of defeat – just!

6

Playing Well to Win

Introduction

This chapter explores the techniques you will need to master if you seriously want to win at playing Scrabble, and are not bothered about the final score you reach. Playing to win – or matchplay Scrabble, as it is more properly called – has now become the dominant form of Scrabble in the UK. The National Scrabble Championship has changed its format to embrace matchplay Scrabble. Scrabble clubs and official tournaments have reverted to matchplay Scrabble. Many players would claim that matchplay Scrabble is truer to the origins of the game than the artificiality of playing for ever-higher scores. In the country where Scrabble originated, the USA, the concept of playing for high scores has never really gained a foothold. Playing to win has always been the style of Scrabble played in the USA.

Matchplay Scrabble is simply about winning. Just because the scores are significantly lower does not mean that there is a lower level of skill involved. Playing matchplay Scrabble well can be even more demanding than playing for high scores! Many of the concepts relevant to matchplay are the same as in high-score Scrabble, while others are just the opposite.

General Principles

Just to repeat the fundamental tenet of matchplay Scrabble: *Winning is all-important*. It does not matter whether your final score is 500 points or 250 points. All you need to ensure is that your final score is higher than your opponent's. Scrabble tournaments often employ the concept of 'spread' in order to break ties between players having the same number of wins. This is explained in more detail in the next section. While playing in any particular game or tournament, you will need to be aware of whether spread is important or not.

In high-score Scrabble, it is important to eke out the Scrabble tiles as long as possible, in order to keep driving the final score onwards and upwards. In practice, this means a series of bonus plays (perhaps nine-timers, even) interspersed with lower-scoring plays and exchanges. In matchplay Scrabble, it is important to keep up an even pattern of scoring throughout the game. You have to keep plugging away, achieving scores of 25, 40, 35, 25 and 40, move after move. You should endeavour never to fall behind your opponent. Once you fall behind, he will make it increasingly difficult for you to score, and you will find yourself unable to catch up with him. Putting this the other way round, you should always try to have the edge on your opponent. Once you are comfortably in the lead – perhaps 40-60 points – you should start blocking the positions where he might expect to make good scores. In a nutshell: keep the board open until you are ahead, and close it down once you are ahead!

The more letters you use on each turn, the more you will pick up, thereby increasing your chances of picking up blanks, S's and the high-value tiles. These are the tiles which will help you get good scores, pull ahead of your opponent, and then start to block the board to hamper the opponent. In high-score Scrabble, you are encouraged to turn over your tiles slowly, except for the bonus plays. In matchplay Scrabble, just the opposite is the case. Try to use as many tiles as possible on each play. Make four- , five- and six-letter words if they score well. The greater your turnover, the lower are the chances of your opponent picking up useful tiles. At the end of a game, if you have played 55-60 tiles, and your opponent has only managed to play 40-45, then the chances are that you will have achieved the higher score.

50-point bonuses still occur in matchplay Scrabble, but their importance is less than in high-score Scrabble. Of course, if you can make a bonus word from your seven tiles, that's fine, but the need to retain good letter combinations (such as AEIRS) in order to make bonuses is much reduced. In order to keep your scoring levels up, you will need to be prepared to play S's and blanks for plays other than bonuses. While this is a simple principle to state, it can be very difficult for some players to put into practice, when they have been used to holding back such tiles for potential bonus plays. More on this later!

In high-score Scrabble, you are encouraged to open up premium squares, especially the 3W squares, in order to boost scores. You are encouraged also to place vowels next to 3L and 2L squares to aid high-scoring from medium- and high-value consonants placed on those squares. The opposite is the case in matchplay Scrabble. Opening up such premium squares will invite your opponent to grab them for an immediate tactical advantage. You should try to minimize the number of premium squares made accessible, especially the 3W ones, and you should always endeavour to use a valuable opened-up premium square before your opponent gets to it!

The Concept of 'Spread'
At officially organized Scrabble tournaments, the winner is the player who has achieved the most wins out of however many games have been played. As it possible that more than one player will have the same number of wins, the concept of 'spread' has gained currency, and is frequently used for breaking ties. Spread is merely the sum of the winning and losing margins in each of your games. For example, if you play three games, winning two of them by 30 and 50 points, and losing one by 10 points, then your spreads in the three individual games are $+30$, $+50$ and -10, giving a total spread of $+70$. If more than one player has the same number of wins, then the highest total spread is used to break the ties.

Where the concept of spread is being used, you will need to ensure that, not only do you win your games, you win them by as large margins (or spreads) as possible. Where spread is used, it is obviously better to win a game by 280 points to 250 points (a spread of $+30$ points), rather than winning by 450 points to 430 points (a spread of only $+20$ points).

Keep Scoring
The aim of matchplay Scrabble is to win. You will achieve this not only by making good scores on your own part, but by denying good scoring opportunities to your opponent. The sooner you can build up a reasonable lead (say, 40-60 points), the sooner you can start blocking the board, ensuring your opponent has nowhere to play a bonus word, nowhere to score 50+ points from an X, and so on. You need to keep up the scoring pressure. You should be aiming for a succession of scores like 25, 30, 35 and 40 points, perhaps interspersed with

an occasional 60+ points for a bonus word. Keep up these sorts of scores, and you will quickly pull away from your opponent. Then you can start blocking the board. Of course, you will need to keep the scoring pressure on, just in case he manages to squeeze in some good moves somewhere.

If you find yourself continually scoring 6, 10 or 15 points, then you are not being aggressive enough. One or two scores like these are acceptable when you are blocking what may be the only available place for your opponent to get a bonus word down. On average, though, you should be scoring 25-30 points for each move.

The Opening Move
In matchplay Scrabble, it is important to have the first move. As the first word played covers a 2W square, you stand a good chance of getting a reasonable score, thereby taking the lead immediately. The pressure is then on your opponent right from the start of the game.

Having the first move is also important because, on average, it will mean you have more turns than your opponent. It is reasonable to assume that the total number of moves is an odd number in 50% of games, and is an even number in the other 50% of games. If you have the first turn in a game, you will get one more turn than your opponent in the odd 50%, and the same number of turns in the even 50%. On average, then, you will get half a turn more than your opponent when you have the first turn. This slight advantage should not be overlooked. Getting the first turn is to be welcomed!

Having got the first turn, don't waste it. Make as strong a play as you can, putting your opponent under instant pressure. Assuming that your first word is played across on row 8 (rather than down in column H), do be aware of the 2L squares at D8 and L8. Can you make a word of at least five letters, with a high- or medium-value letter falling on one or other of these 2L squares? Even a simple word like DOLLY, played from H8a, will score 26 points – see Figure 86. Do be careful though of an initial play like BATCH or PARTY, again from H8a. If your opponent happens to have the ING sequence, he will add this at the right-hand end, thereby reaching the 3W square at O8. If there is the possibility of this sort of move,

Playing Well to Win

then position your BATCH or PARTY slightly differently, taking a few less points, but avoiding the risk of your opponent capitalizing on your play. Perhaps BATCH or PARTY from D8a would be a better choice – see Figure 87. Similarly, watch out for letters that can be added at the front of your word, enabling the opponent to reach the 3W square at A8. If you want to play FINED from D8a as your first word, beware of your opponent adding CON to the beginning of it. Better to play FINED from H8a, with the D covering a 2L square – see Figure 88.

	A	B	C	D	E	F	G	H	I	J	K	L	M	N	O
1	3W			2L				3W				2L			3W
2		2W				3L				3L				2W	
3			2W				2L		2L				2W		
4	2L			2W				2L				2W			2L
5					2W						2W				
6		3L				3L				3L				3L	
7			2L				2L		2L				2L		
8	3W			2L				**D**	**O**	**L**	**L**	**Y**			3W
9			2L				2L		2L				2L		

Figure 86: A first move of DOLLY

	A	B	C	D	E	F	G	H	I	J	K	L	M	N	O
1	3W			2L				3W				2L			3W
6		3L				3L				3L				3L	
7			2L				2L		2L				2L		
8	3W			P	A	R	T	Y				2L			3W
9			2L				2L		2L				2L		

(a) Play PARTY from D8a, rather than ....

	A	B	C	D	E	F	G	H	I	J	K	L	M	N	O
1	3W			2L				3W				2L			3W
6		3L				3L				3L				3L	
7			2L				2L		2L				2L		
8	3W			2L				P	A	R	T	Y			3W
9			2L				2L		2L				2L		

(b) PARTY from H8a ...

	A	B	C	D	E	F	G	H	I	J	K	L	M	N	O
1	3W			2L				3W				2L			3W
6		3L				3L				3L				3L	
7			2L				2L		2L				2L		
8	3W			2L				P	A	R	T	Y	I	N	G
9			2L				2L		2L				2L		

(c) because your opponent may play PARTYING

Figure 87: A first play of PARTY

(a) Play FINED from H8a, rather than ....

(b) FINED from D8a ...

(c) because your opponent may play CONFINED

Figure 88: A first play of FINED

Premium Squares

In high-score Scrabble, it is to the advantage of both players to open up the premium squares, so that either of them can potentially benefit from these squares. Opening up pairs of 3W squares for possible nine-timers is greatly encouraged. The opposite is the case in matchplay Scrabble. Try to avoid providing easy access to a 3W square. Once it is available, the chances are that your opponent will take it. Even the simplest four- or five-letter word is liable to score 20+ points when it covers a red square. And if your opponent is able to use one or two of his medium- and high-value tiles, you could be handing him a very easy 40+ points.

Try to avoid creating nine-timer openings! If you play a word such that one letter is floating part way between two 3W squares, the opponent can be guaranteed to use at least one of the red squares, again picking up a useful 40+ points. If you are unfortunate enough that your opponent manages to play a word stretching across the two red squares, it will net him at least 120 points, and maybe a good deal more. He will then have such a large lead over you that he can afford to spend the rest of the game blocking and wrecking your potential scoring positions. The only time that it is at all reasonable to open up a nine-timer possibility is when you are playing a bonus (or perhaps some other move worth 60+ points) and there is absolutely nowhere else to go. You should cross your fingers very tight, hoping he doesn't have a nine-timer play. And you may just have to grin and bear it when your opponent uses one of the red squares.

Even so, if you are at a stage in the game when you are comfortably ahead, and your opponent is giving signs of being close to a bonus (perhaps he has just exchanged one or two tiles), then it may well be worth denying yourself your own bonus if you can avoid opening up one or two 3W squares. It may be a good deal safer to accept 30 points somewhere, rather than getting your bonus down for 70+ points, and then seeing the opponent get his bonus down for 80+ points.

You are not going to be able to get through a game without providing access to 2W squares. But do be on the lookout for giving your opponent the chance of a four-timer – a word straddling two 2W squares with a convenient floating letter between them. The 2W squares where this occurs are those at E5, K5, E11 and K11.

In high-score Scrabble, you are encouraged to put vowels adjacent to 2L and 3L squares, in anticipation of either player being able to benefit from neatly placed consonants. The opposite reasoning applies to matchplay Scrabble. If you play a word that runs adjacent to a premium square, try to ensure that a consonant sits next to the 2L and 3L squares. Try to minimize the score that your opponent could garner from these premium squares. Figure 73 showed the correct positioning of the word EWE on the first move of a high-score game.

	A	B	C	D	E	F	G	H	I	J	K	
1	3W			2L				3W				
2		2W				3L				3L		
3			2W				2L		2L			
4	2L			2W				2L				
5					2W						2W	
6		3L				3L				3L		
7			2L				2L		2L			
8	3W			2L	**E**	**W**	**E**					
9			2L				2L		2L			

	A	B	C	D	E	F	G	H	I	J	K	
1	3W			2L				3W				
2		2W				3L				3L		
3			2W				2L		2L			
4	2L			2W				2L				
5					2W						2W	
6		3L				3L				3L		
7			2L				2L		2L			
8	3W			2L				**E**	**W**	**E**		
9			2L				2L		2L			

Figure 89: The first move
Above, right! Below, wrong!

Figure 89 shows the correct position for the same word in a matchplay game. Do not put the E's adjacent to the 2L squares at G7, I7, G9 and I9. Make sure the W is adjacent to two of these squares. Do not play EWE from H8a, as it provides a convenient hook (EWER, EWES) for your opponent to reach one or both of the 2W squares at K5 and K11. The correct position for EWE is at F8a. There are no words that can be created by adding a single letter at the front of EWE, so there is no access to the 2W squares at E5 and E11.

Conversely, if your opponent opens up premium squares – 3W squares, four-timer possibilities, nine-timer possibilities, 3L squares adjacent to vowels – then dive in quickly and take them. Score as well as you can from them, and deny them to your opponent. But . . .

Be careful about taking premium squares that in turn may open up other premium squares. Consider the board position shown in Figure 90. Suppose your opponent has a promising rack, such as EIORST*. He has several seven-letter words here, but nowhere to put them on this board. His only hope of playing a bonus is to tempt you to open up a position where a bonus word will go. He decides to play WOO at E11a, opening up the 3W square at H15. You are aware that WOO has several hook possibilities – D, F, L, N, S and T. You are tempted by the red square at H15, and you play a five-letter word from H11. You have now provided an opening for your opponent. Having played an O, he has now picked up another letter – a second I, perhaps. With EIIRST* on his rack, he stands a good chance of playing a bonus around the letter on H15. He might even be able to make his bonus word cover one or other of the 3W squares at A15 and O15.

When the board is sufficiently blocked, as in Figure 90, don't be tempted by set-up plays created by your opponent to work in his favour. You should play elsewhere on the board, still taking care not to open up any bonus or high-scoring positions. If you leave the WOO hook available, your opponent might take it on his next turn for 30+ points, but then opening up the red squares on row 15 for you, perhaps. Alternatively, you could use the WOO hook, but with a word that ends in row 13. For example, BLED at H10d gives nothing away.

	A	B	C	D	E	F	G	H	I	J	K	L	M	N	O
1	3W			2L				3W				2L			3W
2		2W				3L				3L				2W	
3			2W				2L		2L				2W		
4	2L			2W				2L				2W			2L
5					2W						2W				
6		3L				3L		D		3L		F		3L	
7			2L				Q	U	A	G		E	2L		
8	3W			2L	V	I	N		O	O	Z	Y			3W
9			C		P	A			M	O	O		E		
10		V	O	R		P				K	N	O	W	3L	
11			A		W	O					2W	X			
12	2L		C	H	E	R		2L		E	Y	E			2L
13			H	I	E	S	2L		2L	F	U	N	G	I	
14		2W				3L				3L				2W	
15	3W			2L				3W				2L			3W

Figure 90: A blocked board

Now put yourself in your opponent's position. It might be *you* who is close to a bonus word but with nowhere to play it. Be prepared to try and tempt your opponent with a play like WOO. More experienced players are unlikely to fall for it, but there are plenty of players who will snap up the 3W square at H15, thereby giving you the much-needed opening you wanted.

Turnover

As was explained earlier, the greater your turnover, the more chance you will have of picking up blanks, S's and the high- and medium-value tiles. These are the tiles which will help you get good scores. Try to use as many tiles as possible on each play, although not at the expense of scoring, opening up premium squares, or not using already opened premium squares. Make four- , five- and six-letter words if they score well. Knowledge of four-, five- and six-letter words is not especially important in high-score Scrabble, where the emphasis is on words of length two, three, seven and eight. Not so with matchplay Scrabble. You will find that knowledge of the intermediate length words will help you use up unwanted tiles, will help you reach premium squares perhaps five or six rows away, and will, of course, increase your turnover.

The greater your turnover, the poorer the chances of your opponent picking up useful tiles. By the end of a game, if you have played 55-60 tiles, and your opponent has only managed to play 40-45, then the likelihood will be that you will have achieved the higher score.

Rack Balancing

Rack balancing was discussed in the previous two chapters. It is just as sensible to ensure that you have a balanced rack in matchplay Scrabble as it is in high-score Scrabble. Remember, you should strive to keep a balanced rack of vowels and consonants, containing two or three vowels, and four or five consonants. If you have excess vowels on your rack (four or more), try to play off the excess ones. The same goes for consonants. If you can get rid of these excesses, your vowel-consonant distribution will tend to return to a normal balance as you take replacement tiles from the bag.

As with high-score Scrabble, this advice needs to be tempered with any special knowledge you have about a given game. If ten E's have been played on the board in the first half of the game, it might be reasonable to retain the two on your rack for more considered use later on. If an abnormally high number of consonants has been played in the first half of a game, it would be wise to keep back the ones you have, in anticipation of their 'drying up' in the second half of the game.

Although the opportunity for bonus plays is lower in match-play Scrabble than in high-score Scrabble, the same principles apply to finding seven- and eight-letter words. Minimize any duplicate letters. Two blanks, two S's or two E's will not cause problems, but you may find that a pair of other letters reduces your chances of spotting a bonus word. Duplicates and triplicates need using up quickly.

In high-score Scrabble, much emphasis was placed on retaining common letter combinations – the likes of -AGE, -ANT, -ED, -ENT, -IEST, -ING, OUT-, RE- and so on. Although these can be useful to have in matchplay Scrabble, it is not usually worth forgoing a good score merely to keep one of these groupings on your rack. You will find yourself having to break up these letter groups in order to get down a four- or five-letter word which scores 35 points.

Watch out for groups of two and three letters that 'go well' together and which can be used in intermediate length words. You will find it easier to make these words than their seven- and eight-letter cousins needed for high-score Scrabble. Here are some examples:

ACC	CKL	GGY	MMY	PP	TW
BB	CKY	GH	MP	PPY	VIV
BBL	FF	GHT	MPY	RCH	WH
BBY	FFY	IFY	NK	SCH	WR
CH	FL	ITY	NKY	TCH	XY
CK	FR	MM	PH	TH	ZY

Even a seemingly unbalanced rack might contain an odd-looking word capable of getting a reasonable score. There are many useful words which use strange combinations of letters and which can be especially useful for both scoring and returning your rack to a more balanced state. Try to learn some of these sorts of words.

AITU	GHYLL	MPRET	SCHTIK	TYG	WILJA
AWDL	GYMP	MVULE	SHTUMM	TYMP	WYND
BLINTZ	GRYPT	MYRRH	SWOWND	URAO	YMPT
BURQA	GYNY	NAOI	SYNC	VLY	YUFT
EUOI	HWYL	RHY	TEHR	VOZHD	ZIFF
FYRD	MOOI	RYND	TRYP	WAQF	ZOPP

Exchanging Tiles

If your rack has an imbalance that cannot easily or quickly be corrected, then do be prepared to exchange tiles. If you are sitting with IIIIOUU on your rack, you might be able to pick up 12-16 points somewhere from a neatly placed IO or OU, but you will have a similar problem with your next rack, and the one after that. In spite of all the advice about keeping up the pressure on your opponent by continued scoring of 25, 30 and 40 points, there are occasions when you should recognize that you will not recover from a dire rack like this for three or four turns. By which time it may be too late to retrieve the game. Exchange your tiles. In the case of IIIIOUU, quite how many depends on the number of vowels still to come. If there are only seven tiles left in the bag, plus the seven your opponent has, and there are only three vowels among those fourteen, be careful! If you put back all of your vowels, you may just pick up a handful of consonants. In this case, keep back a couple of vowels, and exchange five of them. If you are still in the early or middle stages of a game, though, put back six of the tiles. Retain one vowel, just in case you pick all consonants.

The same considerations apply to an all-consonant rack. With BDFGLMR on your rack, you ought to exchange six or maybe all seven of the tiles. If you exchange six, keep back the R to give yourself some scope just in case you pick all vowels.

With any rack, there is little logic in exchanging fewer than six tiles. If your hand has a reasonable number of tiles worth hanging on to, then you could probably use some or all of them in combination with the letters you were intending to exchange.

If your tiles are so bad that you are prepared to miss a scoring opportunity, then you should maximize your turnover. Ideally exchange all seven tiles, or perhaps hold back just one. A six- or seven-tile exchange will give you the best chances of picking up good tiles from the bag.

Hooks

High-score Scrabble involves the liberal creation of hooks at various positions on the board, in order that both players may benefit by having somewhere to tack their bonus words to.

In matchplay Scrabble, if a hook is played and the extensions are known to both players, then the hook could be used immediately by the other player. If both players know the hook's extensions, then neither has any advantage over the other player.

Some hook words have obvious extensions which both players will be aware of, yet there may be additional extensions known only to one of the players. For example, the word BAP has the obvious extension BAPS. But it also has the strange extension BAPU. The player who originally played the BAP hook is aware that the word will take a U. Assuming no S's or U's have been played already, he has double the probability of using the hook position that his opponent has. If all the S's have been used already, and there is at least one U still to come, then only he will be able to make use of the hook, assuming he picks up a U subsequently.

Of course, just because a player plays a particular hook word, this is no guarantee that he will know all the extensions. In the case of BAP, he may have played the word merely to use up a B and P, scoring 20 + points. He may not be aware of any hook extension other than the obvious BAPS.

The knack of effectively using hook words in matchplay Scrabble comes from (a) setting up hook words with strange extensions, and (b) in applying the extensions. The set-up is playing BAP in the first place, knowing full well that it can become BAPU; changing BAP, regardless of who first played it, to BAPU is applying the extension. The more strange hooks you know, the greater the chance that you rather than your opponent will be able to make use of them. Experienced Scrabble players find it particularly useful to know many obscure hooks.

Two-letter words acting as hooks for three-letter words should be reasonably well-known from high-score Scrabble. But matchplay Scrabble tends to require the use of longer hook words, three-letter words acting as hooks for four-letter words, fours acting as hooks for fives, and so on.

Here are some strange hooks and extensions that could be valuable in your armoury:

(T)AHA	(F)ANON	(N)APRON	(T)ALLOTS
ARE(G)	BARD(O)	(S)CLIFF	ATTAIN(T)
BIT(O)	DOWN(A)	CLIFF(Y)	(P)EERIER
BIT(T)	(A)FOUL	(T)HEAVE	(B)OWNING
DIE(B)	FOUL(E)	(U)LOSES	(F)RABBIT
FAD(O)	(C)HOOF	(T)OCHER	(P)RESTED
GYM(P)	PAYS(D)	(U)PLEAD	SALIVA(L)
LOB(I)	(S)POSH	(D)ROGER	(A)TACTIC
YUK(O)	SNOW(K)	(U)SWARD	TURBAN(D)
(M)ZEE	YOGI(C)	VILLA(R)	ZITHER(N)

If you want to make your own lists of favoured hooks, then *Official Scrabble Lists* methodically documents all the hooks for words of length two to seven letters.

Blanks and S's
Because of the need to keep the pressure on your opponent by continual scores of 25 +, you must be prepared to use any

blanks and S's for considerably less than you might do in a high-score game.

Although blanks and S's can still be very useful in getting bonus words down on the board, you should seriously consider using a blank or an S for a score of 40+ points. Of course, if you can make some other move for roughly the same number of points without having to dispense with your blank or S, then by all means play the move that keeps the blank or S on your rack.

Be quite prepared to use your blank as a U in order to play out the Q, but taking care you still score 40 points or so for it.

50-point Bonuses

50-point bonuses occur less frequently in matchplay games than in high-score games. They are far from being a rarity, though. An experienced Scrabble player might get one or two bonuses in a matchplay game, compared with three or four in a high-score game.

The opportunity for bonuses is less for several reasons. One, it is not always worthwhile to retain blanks and S's until a bonus play comes along. The need to keep scoring means that such tiles are often used for non-bonus plays. Two, retention of low-value letters is less likely in matchplay Scrabble. Such letters tend to get used up quickly in the dash for points. And three, there tend to be fewer openings for bonus words to go down on the board in a matchplay game.

In high-score Scrabble, the seven-letter combination AEINRST frequently appears on players' racks, enabling them to make one of the 10 anagrams of these letters. Yet in matchplay Scrabble, this sequence of letters is seen far less frequently. Players just cannot afford to take the time necessary to build up bonuses. While they are doing this, their matchplay opponent is putting down various moves, which are both lengthening his lead and blocking the available bonus positions on the board.

It is not at all unknown for matchplay games to be won without the winner having played a single bonus word. So, remember: you don't need bonuses to win at matchplay Scrabble! They help, but they are not essential.

Opening and Closing the Board

Remember the message spelled out in at the beginning of this chapter: keep the board open until you are ahead, and close it down once you are ahead!

In letting the board develop, you should ensure that it isn't too open to begin with. The reason for this is that if you manage to pull ahead by 50 points or so after the first third of the game, there may be so many openings on the board for bonus plays and other high-scoring moves that you just will not be able to block all of these openings and deny them to your opponent! In other words, try to keep the board slightly open, but ready to start blocking it as soon as you open up a reasonable lead.

What is meant by 'slightly open'? Take a look at the board shown in Figure 91.

There are a number of openings on this board. The E on H8 provides for the possibility of an eight-letter word from H1d; the floating Q on F6 provides for the possibility of a bonus play; the floating Y on N12 allows for a bonus play from N5d; and TIP is a hook for an I, S and T, allowing for a bonus play on row 14. If, at this stage of the game, it was necessary to start

	A	B	C	D	E	F	G	H	I	J	K	L	M	N	O
1	3W			2L				3W				2L			3W
2		2W				3L				3L				2W	
3			2W				2L		2L				2W		
4	2L			2W				2L				2W			2L
5					2W						2W				
6		3L				Q				3L				3L	
7			2L			U	2L		2L				2L		
8	3W			K	N	I	F	E	D			2L			3W
9			2L	I		E	A		H				2L		
10		Z		N		T	I		O	B				3L	
11		A		G	2W		L		W	E	F	T			
12	2L	G	E	L				2L		D	A	I	L	Y	2L
13			M	Y			2L		2L			P	A		
14		2W				3L				3L				2W	
15	3W			2L				3W				2L			3W

Figure 91: A 'slightly open' board

blocking these openings, they could all be blocked fairly easily. The letter B on H7 would kill off two of the openings, those using the Q and E; the strange word VLY played from N10d would block the Y; and XI at M14a would neutralize TIP as a hook word. Figure 92 shows how three moves and five letters have now blocked the board.

Of course, overzealous blocking can be counterproductive. If the board becomes so blocked that only a few low-scoring plays are possible, you may find that you literally run out of space in a few moves' time. The secret lies in having one or two ways to extend a board if it becomes overly blocked. For example, in Figure 92, the word KINGLY could be extended to become STRIKINGLY or some other word ending in KINGLY. Opening up the board in this way immediately provides three floating letters, the S, T and R, that the opponent might suddenly seize upon. UNKINGLY, with only a single floating letter, the U, provides a more controlled opening up of the board.

What to your opponent looks like a blocked board may not be that at all, if you have seeded it with an appropriate hook

	A	B	C	D	E	F	G	H	I	J	K	L	M	N	O
1	3W			2L				3W				2L			3W
2		2W				3L				3L				2W	
3			2W				2L		2L				2W		
4	2L			2W				2L				2W			2L
5					2W						2W				
6		3L				Q				3L				3L	
7			2L			U	2L	B	2L				2L		
8	3W			K	N	I	F	E	D			2L			3W
9			2L	I		E	A		H				2L		
10		Z		N		T	I		O	B				V	
11		A		G	2W		L		W	E	F	T		L	
12	2L	G	E	L				2L		D	A	I	L	Y	2L
13			M	Y			2L		2L				P	A	
14		2W				3L				3L			X	I	
15	3W			2L				3W				2L			3W

Figure 92: A blocked board

word, with an extension unknown to the opponent. In Figure 92, suppose that the B had not been used to block the floating E and Q. Consider the play of the word QUOTH from F6a. To most opponents, that will still look like a blocked board. However, the fact that QUOTH provides a hook position for the letter A, and only that letter, could be invaluable later on. Of course, you will need to be fortunate enough to have the letters UOTH in order to make that move . . .

Reading Your Opponent's Plays

You may be playing to win, but is your opponent? Perhaps you have come up against an opponent who is playing for a high score, or maybe an opponent who just isn't aware that there are two completely different styles of game, high-score and matchplay. You will quickly need to ascertain what sort of game your opponent is playing.

Is he is playing for high scores, making the sorts of moves described in the last chapter? Is he playing short words, of two and three letters? Is he turning over only a few tiles at a time? Is he conveniently opening up premium squares, especially the 3L and 3W ones? Any hint of a nine-timer set-up? Is he exchanging just a couple of tiles? If the answer to any of these questions is 'yes', then he is probably not playing the same style of game as you! If he is playing a different style of game, then you ought to be able to capitalize on it. His plays of short words and limited exchanges should mean all the more tiles for you. Just because your opponent is not going for a high turnover of tiles is no reason to relax your own turnover. Keep the pressure on! Continue to use as many tiles as you can, perhaps ending up with 60 or so of the tiles in the game. If your opponent makes those valuable 3L and 3W squares accessible, you should be fairly keen to take them yourself. But do just check that you are not handing an even better opportunity to your opponent in the process. Every time your opponent makes an opening – a convenient hook, for example – use it or block it.

The chances are, though, that your opponent *will* be playing a matchplay game, just as eager to win as you are. After each and every play that your opponent makes, don't rush to put your own next word down. Analyse what your opponent has just done. Why did he make the move he did? Was it solely for the score he achieved? Or was it for the turnover? Or did he play a hook word that could be added to later? Was his move a spoiling move, perhaps closing down access to a particular premium square or maybe just closing off access to a particular part of the board? Did he exchange tiles? How many? Was it a move designed to divert your attention from some other part of the board? How can you tell? And does it matter, anyway?

If your opponent managed a fairly respectable score, 25 + points perhaps, then there certainly would have been an element of just taking a reasonable score. Anything less than 20 + points should cause you to query what else lay behind that move.

Did he play off four or more tiles? If so, he is obviously keeping his turnover up. But what were the tiles? Were they mainly vowels, or mainly consonants, or a mix? If vowels or consonants predominated, perhaps he is having rack balance problems.

Did your opponent play a hook word? Did he get a reasonable score for it, or did he accept a lesser score? The lesser score would suggest he might be planning to use the hook extension fairly soon. On the other hand, if he managed to get a reasonable score, perhaps he just played the word as it was the best scoring place he had, merely intending to create a hook position on the off-chance he might need it later.

If he played a hook word, how many letters did he turn over? A low turnover would also suggest that he expects to make use of the hook extension imminently. Think about it. He had seven tiles on his rack, and felt he was close to a bonus, or at least a good-scoring move. He decided to play two tiles, creating a hook word for which he already had the extension letter. By only playing two tiles, he retained a significant degree of control over the make-up of his rack, obviously expecting to make the bonus or high-scoring move on his next turn. A hook word played with perhaps four or more tiles suggests that he is not about to immediately snap up the spot with the right extension letter.

Did the opponent's last move use up an attractive premium square? As a result, did it open up others? Was the net effect of the move to increase or decrease the number and quality of premium squares available? Using one 3W square and opening up a 2L square is hardly increasing the quality of the premium squares available! What about the proximity of the premium squares opened? Maybe the opponent played a four-letter word to reach a 3W square, but this in turn has opened up another 3W square seven columns away. The proximity of the newly available 3W square is poorer than for the 3W square just used. However, do beware of the opponent opening up 3W squares seven rows or columns away. These are prime spots for bonus plays!

Did the opponent's last move effectively block off an area of the board? Figure 92 showed how the use of a word like VLY immediately blocked off the area in the middle right-hand side of the board. This doesn't mean that the game cannot eventually reach that part of the board. It just means that it has been made unavailable for an immediate play. V's are very good for such blocking moves, predominantly because there are no two-letter words with a V. Other good board-blocking letters are C (but watch out for the allowable two-letter word CH). On the left-hand side of the board and the top half of the

	A	B	C	D	E	F	G	H	I	J	K	L	M	N	O
1	3W			2L				3W				2L			3W
2		2W				3L				3L				2W	
3			2W				2L		2L				2W		
4	2L			G				2L				Q			2L
5			V	A	I	N			J		P	I	U		
6		3L		E		O	B		O	B	O		F	3L	
7			2L		S	P	A	R*	R	E	D		O		
8	3W			W	H	E	R	E				2L			3W
9			L	O	O		2L		2L				2L	V	
10		Z		E	X	T	O*	R	T				M	A	
11		E			2W	I	O		E	I	K		A	E	
12	2L	A	R	E			N	2L		G	Y	R	I		2L
13			E	L	E	G	Y		2L				L		
14		2W				3L				3L				2W	
15	3W			2L				3W				2L			3W

Figure 93: A blocked board

board, the letters J, Q and Z can be useful blockers, because there are no two-letter words with these as their second letters. Figure 93 shows how some of these letters have effectively blocked off parts of the board.

The Z on square B10 has denied any development of the board up column A. The J on square I5 has denied access to the 3W square at H1. The V on square N9 has denied any development up column O. The Q on square L4 has denied immediate access to the top right-hand corner of the board. And the G and V on squares D4 and C5 have made access to the top left-hand corner of the board difficult. (There are ways out of these difficulties, but none of them provides an immediate scoring opportunity. For example, JOR could be extended to become MAJOR, GAE could be extended to ALGAE; and the F and O of UFO could be developed to column O, which in turn would provide access to the 3W squares at O1 and O8. Any attempt to do any of these moves would immediately be used – or at least thwarted – by the other player.)

Did your opponent exchange tiles on his last turn? If so, how many? One, two or even three suggests he may be close to a bonus play. Are there any positions for bonuses? You had better start thinking about blocking them, either with spoiling plays or good-scoring plays of your own. If he exchanged four or more tiles, then he probably has rack balance problems, and an immediate bonus seems unlikely.

Occasionally, your opponent may make a move which tempts you into making a particular play. This could be for two reasons. One, he may want you to use that particular position, and, in so doing, you will open up a premium square or some part of the board that was previously inaccessible to him. Two, he may want you to use that particular position in order not to use or block some opening elsewhere on the board which he hopes to use on his next turn. Beware of 'carrot' offerings like this!

All of these considerations ought to go through your mind in response to every play of your opponent. You may protest that this kind of long drawn-out analysis will take too long. But don't worry. Once you get into the swing of it, you will find it usually takes but a fraction of a minute. However, there may be occasions close to the end of a game where the outcome of the game is so finely balanced that you really may have to spend a few minutes trying to work out what your opponent is up to.

Tile Tracking

Tile tracking is far more important in matchplay Scrabble than high-score Scrabble. You really do need to be able to see at a glance at any stage of a game which of the high-value tiles are still unplayed, or how many S's are still to come, or whether there are a disproportionate number of I, O's or whatever still left out. Figures 71 and 72 show score sheets with the letter distribution on them, enabling you to keep track of tiles played.

Many players profess not to bother with tile tracking, because either it takes too long or they invariably make mistakes, reaching the end of a game only to find that their tile-tracking sheet says there are 16 tiles left, when in reality there are seven on each player's rack and none left in the bag. The answer to this is simple: practice makes perfect! If you get into a set routine for each of your moves (playing the tiles, announcing the score, writing it down, working out the running total score, crossing off the letters played, and then taking new tiles from the bag) and similarly after your opponent's moves (confirming the word, checking the score, writing it down, working out the running total, crossing off the letters played), then you find the whole process becomes reasonably slick and accurate.

If you do persist with tile tracking, you may not find it especially helpful for many of your games. These are probably the games where you have won by quite a large spread, and it hasn't been necessary to work out all the possible alternative plays that your opponent might make at the end of a game. However, for that small fraction of games where tile tracking is needed, it can make the difference between winning and losing, and you will be extremely pleased that you have tracked the tiles so quickly and accurately.

End-game Strategy

The approach to the end of the game can be particularly demanding in terms of the analysis it requires. This can be the part of the game where a potential win is thrown away and where victory can be snatched from the jaws of an almost certain defeat.

The end of the game is in sight. There are almost 80 tiles on the board, with a further 20 + still to come. You and your opponent each have seven tiles on your racks, and there are more than seven tiles in the bag, sufficient for you still to exchange if you wish. This will probably be your last chance to exchange, though. Although you cannot see what tiles are on your opponent's rack or in the bag, you can work out what the total set of tiles is from your tile-tracking sheet. Remember to discount those tiles already on your own rack! What tiles are still to come? Anything especially useful – like a blank, or an S, or the X? Or are the remaining tiles all worth only 1 and 2 points? Is there a surfeit of vowels or consonants? Are there still five R's to come, perhaps? Are there any tiles to come that will be especially awkward to use – the Q or a V? Maybe there's nothing particularly odd about the letters you are unable to see.

This stage of the game can be quite difficult, because you are not entirely sure which letters are on your opponent's rack and which are in the bag. The options available to you include playing some of your own tiles and exchanging.

Are your tiles so dire (maybe BGNNNQV) that you have to exchange? If so, then bite the bullet and do it. But what if you have BGNNOVW with the Q still to come? Try avoiding a late exchange which may only make matters worse. In this case, play out only one or two tiles, minimizing your chances of picking up the Q. If it is still in the bag, try to tilt the odds in favour of your opponent getting it. If you do happen to pick the Q, though, is there anywhere on the board that the Q might be playable, a floating I for QI, or a spare AT for QAT, or a floating U?

What are the relative scores? Are you well ahead, say 50 points or more? Or is it less than that? Are you behind? Can you catch up and still win? Or are you so far behind that there is no hope of winning?

If you are well ahead, you need to ensure that you stay there. Is there any chance of your opponent getting a late bonus? If there is, will his score overtake yours? If so, and you can block the bonus position, then do so, even if you have to sacrifice points. It is better to forgo 35 points and accept 12 points if it means your opponent will be stymied for a place to put his bonus. If you had taken the 35, he might have got 65; yet taking the 12 might have forced him to settle for only 25.

If you are comfortably ahead and a late bonus from your opponent will only bring him neck-and-neck with you, then you really ought to be still going all-out for scores. His bonus might score 65, but if you can surround that with a series of 30 and 40 point moves, that should still be enough to keep you ahead.

If you have a comfortable lead and a bonus from your opponent is unlikely, keep going for the respectable scores. If you are going to win anyway, you need to boost your winning spread.

Suppose you are ahead, but only by a few points – perhaps 20 or so. Your opponent is breathing down your neck, and a late bonus from him is a possibility. This is when you need to maximize your scoring and blocking at the same time! How likely are some of the positions to be used? If one of them necessitates your opponent's use of a floating W, or some other awkward letter, you should perhaps turn your attention to other bonus positions and try to block those. By a particularly clever positioning of your next word, you might be able to block two or more bonus positions in one fell swoop!

You are still ahead by 20 or so points, but there is nothing to suggest a late bonus from your opponent. As ever, go for the best score you can get, but make absolutely sure that you open up no premium squares or any inaccessible parts of the board which could be of value to your opponent.

Even if you have no hope of winning, you may still wish to minimize the other player's winning spread. Better to lose by 70 points than 100 points. All the points made above are just as relevant.

While there are still tiles in the bag available for replenishment, you should try to ensure that you never take the last tiles from the bag. The player who takes the last tiles from the bag often finds himself with more tiles on his rack than the other player, thereby reducing his chances of going out first. If there are two tiles left in the bag, unless there are good reasons to take both of them, try to take just one of them. If there are three tiles in the bag, take two, thereby ensuring your opponent gets the last one. (If you take one of the remaining three, your opponent will then take one, still leaving you with the last tile.)

Suppose the end-game has progressed a little further. Both players have tiles on their racks, but there are none left in the bag. The situation gets a little easier now. You should now have perfect knowledge of your opponent's tiles, and you no longer have the option of exchanging. In this situation, ask yourself what moves are available to the opponent? Can he go out ahead of you? What moves do you have? Can you go out ahead of your opponent?

Don't forget that the first player out benefits by his own score being increased by the face-value of the tiles remaining on the opponent's rack, and the opponent's score is reduced similarly. Bearing this in mind, does the opponent have a particularly awkward letter that will only go out in one place? If so, block it. Conversely, if you have high-value or awkward letters, try to play them out as soon as you can, in order to minimize the chances of your opponent going out with an unexpected play and catching you with an F and V on your rack perhaps.

If one or some of your possible moves are thwarted by your opponent's play, then what can you do? Can you open up any premium squares that your opponent will not be able to use or spoil, because he doesn't have the appropriate letters? This is where a good knowledge of hooks and their extensions is worthwhile. You should try to play a word that you can extend, and which your opponent can neither extend nor block.

Don't forget: winning is important, but you shouldn't neglect your winning or losing spread either.

Sample Matchplay Games
As with a real game of high-score Scrabble, so too with a real game of matchplay Scrabble. Putting all this advice on match-play Scrabble into operation can pose a difficult task. In a real

game, you will not necessarily get the opportunity of doing or even considering all the points discussed here. Your attempts at rack balancing may not be successful. Your tile exchanges may not bring you the tiles you are seeking. Your opponent may have what seems to be an unusual amount of luck in getting blank tiles and bonus moves. All your cleverly played hooks were used or blocked by your opponent. Your analysis of the end-game situation may have been faulty.

However, what might a matchplay game look like where most of these factors were relevant at some point during the game? Two sample games are shown here. Figure 94 shows the final board layout of a matchplay game that you might have played; and Figure 95 is a record of the individual moves and scores achieved by you and your opponent during the game. Figures 96 and 97 record a second matchplay game.

Various comments concerning each of the moves are also given. What better plays were missed? What other considerations should have been made? Should you have scored better? Was your turnover too low? Was your rack balancing all it should have been? Should you have exchanged more often? Less often? What about your opponent's moves? What did he miss? Should he have won? If not, how much closer could he have got to your score?

Sample Matchplay Game (No. 1)

	A	B	C	D	E	F	G	H	I	J	K	L	M	N	O
1	O	D		J			V	A	L	I	D	2L	O	H	O
2	W	E		I		Z				T	O	Q	U	E	S
3		C	O	N	V	E	X		2L		O	U*	R	N	
4	2L	E		N		S	I	B				E			2L
5		N			2W	T		U		O	U	P			
6		T		B	A	Y		N	E	F				3L	
7			K	O	W		2L	T	A			G			
8	D			H	E	A	P	Y				2L	R		3W
9	A		2L			G	2L		2L				I		
10	R	3L				G				3L	S	I	T	3L	
11	I				2W	R		E	L	F	E	D			
12	C	L	U	M	S	I	E	R		A	E	2W			2L
13			T	A	I		M	A	R		N		2W		
14		2W				3L	E	S*		3L				2W	
15	3W			2L				3W				2L			3W

Figure 94: The board in a sample matchplay game (No. 1)

You

Tiles	Move	Score	Total
AEHIPRY	D8a, HEAPY	34	34
ABIIRVY	D6a, BAY	30	64
IIILRVX	G3d, XI	34	98
IIILRUV	(exchange IIILRUV)	0	98
CEEFNOS	H6a, NEF	14	112
CENOPSU	J5a, OUP	15	127
CEIJMNS	D1d, JINN	38	165
CELMRSU	A12a, CLUMSIER	82	247
EELOOTU	J2a, TOQUE	32	279
EEHILOO	M1a, OHO	25	304
DEEFILO	H11a, ELFED	20	324
AAEIIOT	J12a, AE	9	333
AAIILOT	C13a, TAI	16	349
AAILNOS	K10d, SEEN	6	355
AAILNOR	H7a, TA	6	361
AILNOR	K3a, OURN	22	383
AIL		−3	380

Your Opponent

Tiles	Move	Score	Total
EEKOSTW	C7a, KOW	25	25
BEESTTZ	F2d, ZESTY	37	62
BEINTTU	H4d, BUNTY	21	83
DEEEIIT	(exchange DEEIIT)	0	83
CDENORV	B3a, CONVEX	36	119
DEEGQR*	L2d, QUEP (U = blank)	28	147
DEGGIIR	F8d, AGGRI	11	158
ADDDEIR	A8d, DARIC	24	182
DDEENOT	B1d, DECENT	22	204
ADILORV	G1a, VALID	32	236
EIMORSW	A1d, OW	29	265
AEIMRRS	G13a, MAR	19	284
EGIIRS*	L10d, ID	3	287
EGIRST*	O1d, OS	17	304
EGIRT*	M7d, GRIT	11	315
E*	G14a, ES (S = blank)	9	324
		3	327

Figure 95: The racks and moves in a sample matchplay game (No. 1)

Comments on Matchplay Game 1

your moves   **your opponent's moves**

AEHIPRY: HEAPY is better than HARPY as it leaves a vowel and consonant (IR) rather than two vowels (EI). There are no vowels adjacent to the 2W squares at G7 and G9.

> **EEKOSTW**: This scores well. The rack leave of EEST is fine – duplicate E's are unlikely to be a problem. Note that there is no hook extension at the beginning of KOW.

ABIIRVY: Various possibilities here: E9a,BRA,21 – leaving IIVY; H4d,VAIRY,15 – leaving BIY; G8d, PRIVY,14 – leaving ABI (this opens up the 3W square at H15). All of these leave poor selections of letters on the rack. On balance, BAY is probably best. Note that BAY provides a hook position for the letters E, S and T. Note that AWE also provides a hook position for a W – WAWE. The rack leave of IIRV might become a problem.

> **BEESTTZ**: BEZ from F5a would score 21 points. Could also play ZESTY at either of H4d (27) or F2d (37); could also play ZEES at G3d (32), but ZEES is a hook for an M, MZEES. The Z on G3 also opens up the 3W square at H1. Play ZESTY for 37 points, even though it uses the S.

IIILRVX: G3d,XI,36 scores well, but doesn't give a good turnover. However, there doesn't appear to be an attractive way of playing two I's and two of the consonants, and getting a good score. F3a,ELIXIR,22 is possible, but opens up the 3W square at H1, as well as putting a vowel beneath the 3L square at J2. Note that EX does not provide a hook to give access to H1. One good feature of playing XI is that it blocks the floating Z, E and S of ZESTY.

> **BEINTTU**: No seven-letter anagram here. A floating D or S would give UNBITTED and BUNTIEST, but there aren't any floating D's or S's. Playing BUNTY or BUTTY both provide good tile turnover and good rack retention (EIT or EIN). G6d,TUP,15 scores too few points and provides too little turnover.

IIILRUV: E3a,VEX,13 scores too few points and only uses one tile. D2a,LUZ,12 has the same problems. There don't seem to be any

plays which score well and turn over several letters. Not a single
tile is especially worth keeping. Therefore, exchange all seven
tiles.

DEEEIIT: Too many vowels here, and duplicate vowels at that.
I5d,TEE,11 scores too few points and still leaves the imbalanced
rack of DEII. E9a,DI,13 leaves an even more imbalanced rack.
F8d,AIDE,9 is a feeble scoring move, and opens up a four-timer.
The same goes for H6a,NIDE,9. In the absence of any worthwhile options, an exchange is in order. It's worth retaining a
single E just in case all consonants are picked up.

CEEFNOS: The S here gives the opportunity of opening up the
board a little. H6a,NEF,14 leaves a quite reasonable rack of
CENOS, with NEF only taking an S at the end. The floating F
doesn't give away much.

CDENORV: There are no seven- or eight-letter words with these
letters. B3a,CONVEX,36 provides excellent turnover, good use
of the X, excellent tile retention (DER), and doesn't open up any
3W squares. A good all-round play.

CENOPSU: The anagram here is POUNCES, but it won't go down
anywhere. There are no eight-letter words from the A and P of
HEAPY, either. K2d,COUPS,25 would leave EN. But J5a,OUP
leaves an S hook and a floating P.

DEEGRQ*: The opponent's play of OUP for 15 points looks
suspiciously open. He's probably got good letters. There is little
choice but to play QUEP, using the blank as a U. This provides
no hooks.

CEIJMNS: K3a,JUICE,26 opens up a nine-timer and leaves the
imbalanced MNS on the rack. D1d,JINN,38 is an attractive move.
Although it opens up the 3W square at A1, there will only be a
few possibilities – four- or five-letter words with J as the fourth
letter. Possibilities include BENJ, HADJ, BANJO, BUNJE, GANJA,
NINJA, OUIJA and so on – probably less than 20 all told.

DEGGIIR: Duplicate G's and I's need to be resolved here. Will
any of DIGGER, RIGGED and RIGID go down anywhere? The
opponent is beginning to open up a lead, therefore need to open
up the board in an attempt to get good tiles and some good
scores. F8d,AGGRI,11 is a poor score, but it does give good
turnover and a good rack of retained letters (DEI). An exchange
of tiles did not seem justified.

your moves   **your opponent's moves**

CELMRSU: No seven-letter anagrams here, although the non-existent MUSCLER comes to mind! The floating I on F12 enables both CLUMSIER and MUSCLIER to be played, although both open up a nine-timer position. But it's obvious the opponent is having difficulties – his previous move had a high turnover and a low score. The chances are that the opponent will not have a nine-timer, but will almost certainly take one or other of the 3W squares opened up. Even though a nine-timer place is being opened up, the bonus cannot be forgone at this stage.

> **ADDDEIR**: A surfeit of D's! A12d,CARD,21 will leave DDEI on the rack, as well as providing a bonus possibility from A15. L2a,QADI,28 leaves DDER and opens up another nine-timer position. A8d,DARIC,24 provides turnover, uses the 3W square at A8, denies instant access to the 3W square at A15, and leaves the not too awkward DDE on his rack.

EELOOTU: Too many vowels. J2a,TOQUE,32 gives a good score from the already-played Q, good turnover, and a balanced rack leave (ELO). TOQUE provides a hook for an S, although not for any other letters. Note that two S's and one blank have been used already.

> **DDEENOT**: The only anagram here is DENOTED, but it won't go down anywhere. There are no eight-letter words through the floating E of TOQUE or the floating G of AGGRI. Is TOQUED allowable? Not sure! There are no plays possible reaching the 3W square at H1. M1a,NOD,16 is about the highest score that can be achieved from the 3W square at O1. B1d,DECENT,22 provides a reasonable score and a good turnover.

EEHIOOL: 75 points ahead! Time to start blocking. The R on square H12 provides a possibility for a bonus word played from H11a or H13a, but it's not easy to see how to block it. The TOQUE(S) hook also needs disabling. The play of OHO scores well and effectively blocks TOQUES, but does leave a rather imbalanced EEIL.

> **ADILORV**: 100 points behind! There are no seven- or eight-letter words with these letters. G1a,RIVAL,28 and G1a,VIRAL,28 are both good moves. But better still is G1a,VALID,32. Neither the floating G nor the R of CLUMSIER is blocked by this move.

your moves   **your opponent's moves**

DEEFILO: Check the openings. Decide what is best to block. OUP provides a hook for an S. The R of CLUMSIER will be useful to place various vowels above and beneath. The floating G of AGGRI needs to be made difficult to use. The play of H11a,ELFED,20 is interesting. It makes the R of CLUMSIER harder to use, although ER now provides a hook position for A, E, F, G, N and S. ELFED has no hook posssibilities at the end. A seven-letter bonus beginning with an S on square M5 is now impossible, although a bonus with S as the second letter is a possibility. ELFED has provided three floating letters, F, E and D.

> **EIMORSW**: A floating T would provide for WORMIEST. But there is no T. The play of WO is away from the areas where bonuses might go, in an attempt to keep those areas uncluttered.

AAEIIOT: J12a,AE,9 is a low score, but it does block the three floating letters of ELFED. Note that there is no hook possibility at the end of AE, thereby completely blocking any eight-letter bonus through the D. Note that it is still possible to play a bonus in row 13, given the right letters.

> **AEIMRRS**: The anagrams are MARRIES and SIMARRE, but neither will go down anywhere. N5d,SIMARRE was a possibility until ELFED blocked it. G13a,MARRIES was also a possibility until AE blocked it. There are no particularly difficult letters still to come – all 2 points or less. A bonus is still a possibility, but how? Is it possible to open up two bonus positions on one move? G13a,MAR,19 creates possibilities for a bonus ending on square G14 and one starting on square I14.

AAIILOT: Cannot block both the M and R of MAR. Could do G13a,MART,12 – but even this would allow a bonus to go down with the right letters. Chances are that the opponent has an S or a blank or both! OUP is still a possibility for a seven-letter word with S as the second letter. C13a,TAI,16 certainly makes things awkward on row 13, though still not entirely impossible. At this stage, rack balance and turnover are of secondary importance. Effort must be concentrated on blocking the opponent's possible bonus, while continuing to score some points.

your moves   **your opponent's moves**

> **EGIIRS***: The blank, but probably too late. One of the duplicate I's needs to be played. L10,ID,3 merely provides an opening for a possible bonus to be played on row 9. The R of MAR is still intact for a bonus beginning with an E.

AAILNOS: K10d,SEEN,6 blocks two of the openings for a bonus. SEEN provides no hook possibilities at either end, so row 9 is no longer available for a bonus. The R of MAR is also blocked now.

> **EGIRST***: Several anagrams of these letters, but nothing that will go down on the board. Is there an eight-letter word beginning with OS-, playable from square O1d? After some thought, no! Resigned to the fact that no bonus word is going to be playable, he opts for the score achieved by playing the S on to TOQUE.

AAILNOR: The opponent has EGIRT*. He could go out with J7a,TIGERS,13. That seems to be the only place he can go out in one move. Block it.

> **EGIRT***: Cannot go out in one move, so plan to do it in two.

AILNOR: The opponent now has only E* left, so will be able to go out on his next turn. There are several places, so there is little point in blocking. Need to use up as many tiles as possible, yet scoring reasonably well at the same time. K3a,OURN,22 does nicely.

> **E***: Several low-scoring possibilities. G14a,ES,9 is the best of a poor selection. The opponent is caught with AIL still on his rack.

Sample Matchplay Game (No. 2)

	A	B	C	D	E	F	G	H	I	J	K	L	M	N	O
1	3W			V	I	N*	T	A	G	E	D	2L			W
2		2W		E		3L		B		X	I			2W	O
3			2W	N			G	U	2L				B		M
4	2L			T*			U	S				L	O		E
5			R	A	I		T	E	F		P	A	R	E	R
6		3L		I		3L	T		O	3L	O	W	N	3L	A
7			2L	L			A	C	H		U	N	2L		
8	3W			S				A	N	G	R	Y		E	3W
9			2L				2L	V	2L				2L	O	
10		3L	C			Z	E	E		3L		J		N	
11			O		H	E		M	I	L	I	E	U	S	
12	2L		T	R	O	A	T	E	D			R			2L
13		A	T		D			I	N	2L		K	E	F	
14	Q	I	S			3L					3L	Y		A	D
15	3W	L		2L				3W				2L		P	O

Figure 96: The board in a sample matchplay game (No. 2)

You				Your Opponent			
Tiles	**Move**	**Score**	**Total**	**Tiles**	**Move**	**Score**	**Total**
AGNOORY	H8a, ANGRY	26	26	ACLMNNW	L4d, LAWNY	22	22
ADOOPRU	K5d, POUR	27	53	CEEMNNV	H7d, CAVEMEN	15	37
ADORTTT	C12a, TROATED	16	69	BENRUUZ	F10d, ZEA	32	69
DFHHIOT	E11d, HOD	24	93	ABNORUU	M3d, BORN	25	94
FHIOTV*	I5d, FOHN	25	118	ABEESUU	H1d, ABUSE	29	123
DEGITV*	D1a, VINTAGED (N = blank)	66	184	EEEIILU	H11a, MILIEU	19	142
GJKMRTY	L10d, JERKY	38	222	EEFIINX	J2a, XI	53	195
ADGMTTU	G3d, GUTTA	31	253	EEEFINS	L13a, KEF	20	215
ACDIMOO	N14a, AD	16	269	EEINOPS	N15a, PO	29	244
CIMOOTW	C10d, COTT	12	281	AEEILNS	K5a, PARE	6	250
AEIMORW	O1d, WOMERA	43	324	AEILNS*	D1d, VENTAILS (T = blank)	74	324
IIIIQRS	A14a, QIS	31	355	AEELNOS	B13d, AIL	5	329
IIIR	C5a, RAI	6	361	EENOS	N8d, EONS	15	344
II	G13a, IN	6	367	E	F10a, ZEE	12	356
I		−1	366			1	357

Figure 97: The racks and moves in a sample matchplay game (No. 2)

Comments on Matchplay Game 2

your moves   **your opponent's moves**

AGNOORY: ANGRY seems to be the only word which gets the Y on a 2L square, even though it leaves duplicate O's on the rack.

> **ACLMNNW:** Too many consonants here! CANNY and WANLY are possibilities, but LAWNY is better. Playing WANLY makes it very easy to score off the W in columns K and M. LAWNY makes it more difficult to score off the W in column M, although it will be just as easy to score off it in column K.

ADOOPRU: Probably one vowel too many. Could play POOR or POUR from K5d. ADOR is a slightly better group of letters to retain than ADRU, so play POUR.

> **CEEMNNV:** Still too many consonants! The C, M and V are awkward together, and the duplicate N's are a nuisance. Could just play J6a,VOW,17, but this turns over too few letters. Could play MEVE from E7a or E9a, but both provide access to the 3W square at A8. CAVEMEN achieves the best turnover possible without exchanging, and gets a reasonable score. The floating E, M, E and N could be risky, though.

ADORTTT: What a dreadful pick-up, three T's. TROATED clears out all the letters except for a single T. The T, R, O and A are all risky floaters.

> **BENRUUZ:** This has the makings of a good rack, except for the two U's. F10a,ZEE,32 scores well, but provides a useful hook for MZEE, and does nothing to solve the U problem. E11d,BONZE,32 turns over more tiles, still doesn't tackle the U problem, and sets up a nine-timer possibility. Steer clear of that. On balance, go for F10d,ZEA,32 – at least it gets a reasonable score, and doesn't give away too much.

DFHHIOT: Could do I6a,DHOW,19 – but that only uses two tiles. Or perhaps I5d,FOHN,25 – but that opens up the 3W square at H1. Play safe with E11d,HOD,24. Could always do FOHN next time, given an E, I or O to hook on to the F.

> **ABNORUU:** Can't seem to shake the U's. M3d,BORN turns over four tiles. Could do BARN in the same place. There's little to choose between them. The retention of AUU is not good. Perhaps an exchange will be necessary next time.

FHIOTV*: A blank! I5d,FOHN,25 is still possible. If the opponent takes the 3W square at H1, then perhaps there will be sufficient floaters on the board to enable a bonus play to go down. Could well be worth letting the opponent take the 3W square.

> **ABEESUU**: Five vowels now. Could do H1d,ABUSE,29 points. That provides good turnover, gets rid of one of the U's, leaving just EU on the rack.

DEGITV*: The two most useful floaters are the A and S of ABUSE. There doesn't seem to be anything useful with the S, but there are DIVAGATE and VINTAGED through the A. Take VINTAGED as it gets the V on a 2L square, and scores slightly better.

> **EEEIILU**: The vowels are back with a vengeance! Might be able to play LIEU somewhere, but even that will leave three vowels on the rack. Perhaps an exchange is called for. But how about MILIEU, using the M of CAVEMEN? It notches up a few points, and provides a good turnover. The retention of EE isn't too painful.

GJKMRTY: Apart from the Y, no vowels. This would almost necessitate an exchange, if it wasn't for the floating E in MILIEU. L10d,JERKY,38 is the obvious move. It scores well and turns over four tiles.

> **EEFIINX**: MILIEU takes an X. N10d,EXINE,44 is a nice move, but opens up the 3W squares at O8 and O15. Too risky! Even though it achieves less turnover, J2a,XI scores better and doesn't open up 3W squares.

ADGMTTU: Possibilities are: C4a, GUTTAS, 14; C9d, GUTTA,16; G3d,MUTT,24. But best of all is G3d,GUTTA,31. This leaves DM on the rack.

> **EEEFINS**: 58 points behind. A bonus is needed to catch up. The floating V and I in row 1 and the floating T at C12 all look potentially useful for an eight-letter bonus. Bear in mind that MILIEU also takes an S. Perhaps use up the EF, retaining EEINS. Could do L13a,KEF,20 – although this blocks the MILIEUS hook, it does provide a KEFS possibility. Could do E6a,EFT,14. This messes up the floating V and I, but provides a hook possibility for DEFT, HEFT, LEFT, REFT and WEFT. On balance, go for KEF.

your moves   **your opponent's moves**

ACDIMOO: 38 points ahead. KEF looks very suspicious. The opponent probably has an S or a blank. The position needs blocking. The floating V, I and T are risky, too, but they can wait until next time. N14a,AM,18 makes KEFS more difficult, but a nine-timer ending in -ISMS could still be a possibility. N14a,AD,16 scores less, but is a much better blocking play.

> **EEINOPS**: PEONIES is the only word from these letters, but it won't go in anywhere. N5d,PEONIES is almost possible, but OWNE doesn't exist. And there doesn't seem to be anything using the floating V, I and T. N15a,PO,29 scores well, and still leaves the bonus possibilities open.

CIMOOTW: 25 points ahead. The bonus openings must be blocked. An eight-letter word from the V and an eight-letter word through the T could both be blocked if there was a five-letter word beginning with C playable from C8d. (COMIT would do the job, but isn't a real word.) Anyway, even that doesn't block the floating I. C10d,COTT,12 blocks the T nicely, though. COTT also provides a hook for an A – COTTA. Bear that in mind for later. There is still the possibility of a seven-letter word ending in H, playable from D4d. But that's more unlikely than a word through the T. Take care of the V and I next time.

> **AEEILNS**: No seven-letter words here. The most likely place for a bonus is from the V. VASELINE fits the bill, but is almost certainly spelled with a capital letter. Could it be a verb, with the V perhaps a lowercase letter? Unlikely. Leave the V and I openings. Set up another opening somewhere else, so that the other player is unable to block them all. K5a,PARE,6 provides a hook position for D, O, R, S and U. How many of those will the other player know?

AEIMORW: PARE is too convenient a hook, especially since it was played for a mere 6 points. It needs blocking. O1d,MOWER,40 is the easiest play to spot. WOMERA is a good word to find, but would have scored better at O4d, making PAREO at the same time. Perhaps PAREO wasn't known. The retention of a single I could be useful, since the Q is still to come. The I might be useful for playing QI somewhere.

> **AEILNS***: VENTAILS is the only eight-letter possibility from the floating V. COTT takes an A. Any chance of a word on row 14

your moves   **your opponent's moves**

with the pattern --A-S--? Can't see anything. Even if there was,
VENTAILS would probably still be the better play. Play VENTAILS.

IIIIQRS: Neck and neck on points, but four I's! There are no tiles
left in the pool, so the opponent has AEELNOS. The best play
seems to be A14a,QIS,31. At least the opponent doesn't have an
I for the move A14d,QI. There can't be too many occasions
when it's worth having all the remaining I's. This 31-point score
should be sufficient to win the game, even with the clutch of I's.

> **AEELNOS**: The other player has IIIR, so won't be going out
> quickly. A14d,QI is the obvious next play, so that will need
> blocking. B13d,AIL only scores 5 points, but does stop the other
> player picking up another 33 points.

IIIR: The opponent has EENOS left. Possible plays are:
J1d,EXES,11; F10a,ZEE,12; N8d,EONS,15; and E3d,EONS,17.
Block the best of these with C5a,RAI,6.

> **EENOS**: N8d,EONS,15 will leave a single E for F10a,ZEE,12.

II: The opponent has one E left. Can't do anything to make it
unplayable. Play an I for 6 points.

> **E**: Play ZEE as planned. The other player is caught holding just
> an I, so the scores are adjusted by -1 and +1. The other guy
> wins 366 to 357.

7

Word Knowledge and Word Lists

Introduction
If you want to play Scrabble well, whether playing for high scores or to win, you will need to arm yourself with an extensive vocabulary. While a good general knowledge of words is a useful starting point, you will need to absorb and use the numerous esoteric words that exist in *The Chambers Dictionary* and *Official Scrabble Words*. You will need to know *all* the two-letter words. You ought to try to learn as many as possible of the 1000+ three-letter words. You ought to come to grips with the four- and five-letter words containing a J, Q, X or Z. And so on! Each of the various categories is examined in further detail here.

Two-letter Words
This is a complete list of the 100+ two-letter words appearing in *Official Scrabble Words* (Third Edition). Against each word is a short definition.

A Complete List of Two-Letter Words

Word	Meaning
aa	Type of volcanic rock
ad	An advertisement
ae	Scots form of 'one'
ah	To make an interjection of surprise
ai	Three-toed sloth
am	Part of the verb 'to be'
an	Indefinite article
ar	The letter R
as	In whatever manner
at	Denoting position
aw	Interjection of disgust
ax	To cut down
ay	Yes

Word	Meaning
ba	Soul, in ancient Egyptian religion
be	To exist
bi	Person attracted to both sexes
bo	Familiar term of address for a man
by	Near to
ch	Obsolete form of the pronoun 'ich' (I)
da	A Burmese knife
di	Gods, a plural of 'deus'
do	To perform
ea	A river
ee	Scots form of 'eye'
ef	The letter F
eh	To express enquiry
el	An elevated railroad
em	The letter M
en	The letter N
er	Expressing hesitation
es	The letter S
ex	A person's former husband or wife
fa	A musical note
fy	Interjection of disgust
gi	A judo costume
go	To proceed
gu	A kind of violin
ha	An interjection of surprise
he	A male
hi	An interjection calling attention
ho	Cessation
id	Part of the personality
if	A condition
in	To enclose
io	A cry of triumph
is	Part of the verb 'to be'
it	A pronoun
jo	A beloved one
ka	The spirit or soul within a person
ko	a Maori digging-stick
ky	Cows
la	A musical note
li	A Chinese unit of distance
lo	Look!
ma	Mother
me	A musical note
mi	A musical note

Word	*Meaning*
mo	More
mu	A letter of the Greek alphabet
my	Belonging to me
na	A Scots form of 'no'
ne	An obsolete form of 'not'
no	A denial
nu	A letter of the Greek alphabet
ny	An obsolete spelling of 'nigh'
ob	An objection
od	A kind of force
oe	A grandchild
of	Belonging to
oh	An interjection of surprise
oi	An interjection used to attract attention
om	A symbol intoned as part of a Hindu chant
on	To put on
oo	A Scots form of 'wool'
or	The tincture gold or yellow
os	A bone
ou	An interjection expressing concession
ow	An interjection expressing concession
ox	The common domestic cattle
oy	A grandchild
pa	Father
pH	A number used to express the acidity or alkalinity of chemical solutions. (Although the Scrabble rules bar the use of words with initial capital letters, they say nothing about words having capital letters elsewhere!)
pi	A letter of the Greek alphabet
po	A chamberpot
qi	An individual person's life-force, the free flow of which in the body is believed to ensure physical and spiritual health
re	A musical note
sh	Hush!
si	A musical note
so	A musical note
st	Hush!
ta	Thank you

Word	Meaning
te	A musical note
ti	A musical note
to	In the direction of
ug	To feel loathing
um	An interjection used to express hesitation
un	A dialect form of 'one'
up	To raise
ur	An interjection used to express hesitation
us	The objective case of 'we'
ut	A musical note
we	The plural of 'I'
wo	An exclamation of grief
xi	A letter of the Greek alphabet
xu	A coin of Vietnam
ye	An archaic spelling of 'the'
yo	An interjection calling for effort
yu	A precious jade
zo	A hybrid domestic cattle of the Himalayas

Since use of two-letter words is so important to the game, it really is essential that you know all of these. Since many of them are everyday words, you need only concentrate on learning the unfamiliar ones. The brief definitions may help you.

Three-letter Words

Three-letter words are important because (a) they provide the material which allows a two-letter word to be extended by one letter, as you play a word perpendicular to the two-letter specimen, and (b) they are a convenient way of using up two or three letters from your rack that you don't wish to hold.

Official Scrabble Words contains over 1100 three-letter words, ranging from everyday specimens such as ACE, BAD and CAT to exotica such as DSO, ETH and FRA. Of course, it isn't necessary to learn 1100 three-letter words. Many of them will be familiar to you as everyday words. It is only the unfamiliar ones that you need to try and absorb. It might help to distinguish between those which are made by adding a single letter to a two-letter word and those which cannot be created in this way.

For example, EGO can be viewed as an E added to GO, and
HEW can be thought of as a W added to HE; while AFT and COG
cannot be created by the addition of a single letter to a two-
letter word. You will find that the three-letter words composed
of a two-letter word plus another letter occur more frequently
than the other type.

Some three-letter words can be created by adding a letter at the
beginning of a two-letter word or at the end of another two-letter
word. For example, ARE can be viewed as A plus RE, as well as AR
plus E; and OBA can be thought of as O plus BA, as well as OB plus
A. These three-letter words, where the first two letters and the last
two letters are both two-letter words, occur with considerable
regularity in Scrabble. If you are only going to learn a subset of
the three-letter words, this is the group to concentrate on.

J-Q-X-Z Words
In order to squeeze the most value from any of these letters,
you will find it helpful to have an extensive knowledge of short
words – up to five letters – that use any one of these high-value
letters. If you want to play better Scrabble, then you will need
to know and feel comfortable with specimens such as these:

BAJU	QOPH	CALX	AZAN
JIAO	QUEY	FAIX	FOZY
PUJA	QUOP	OXER	PUTZ
BUNJE	BURQA	CULEX	AZINE
LAPJE	MAQUI	IXTLE	GONZO
WILJA	SQUEG	XYSTI	WEIZE

Official Scrabble Lists contains lists of J-Q-X-Z words ranging
from two to eight letters long.

Hooks and Non-hooks
Hooks were introduced at the end of Chapter 4. While it would
be very ambitious to attempt to learn all, or even most, of the
hooks, you should try to learn some of them. *Official Scrabble
Lists* contains extensive lists of hooks. Pick off a few words
and try to learn the relevant hooks. For example, try to
familiarize yourself with the hooks for ANT. The less obvious
ones have been highlighted.

BANT	**LANT**	**ANTA**
CANT	PANT	**ANTE**
DANT	RANT	**ANTI**
GANT	**VANT**	ANTS
KANT	WANT	

Try another example, HOW. Again, the less obvious ones have been highlighted.

CHOW	**HOWE**
DHOW	**HOWF**
SHOW	**HOWK**
WHOW	HOWL
	HOWS

Trying to learn the hooks for a few words at a time should prove more successful than trying to memorize page after page of hooks.

The heading to this section made mention of 'non-hooks'. Not only does it pay to know the valid hook possibilities for a particular word (for example, ANT to BANT), it also helps if you can be confident about invalid hook possibilities. When an opponent quite boldly adds an F to the beginning of ANT, you ought immediately to challenge it, confident in the knowledge that FANT is not an allowed word.

Vowel Dump Words
You will often find that you have too many vowels on your rack. In an attempt to return to a balanced rack of letters, you will find it useful to know words which use an excessive number of vowels, allowing you to play off your unwanted ones. Examples of such words include:

AIA	EALE	INIA	AECIA	ACEDIA
EAU	EUGE	KAIE	AINEE	EIDOLA
AINE	EUOI	LUAU	AULOI	FOVEAE
AMIE	EVOE	MOOI	AUREI	OCREAE
AULA	IDEE	PAUA	OIDIA	SEMEIA
CIAO	ILEA	UNAU	ZOEAE	UREMIA

There are many others that could be added to this short list. Vowel dump words up to eight letters long are listed methodically in *Official Scrabble Lists*.

Consonant Dump Words

Just as it's useful to know words for dumping excessive vowels, so too is it useful to know words for dumping excessive consonants. A few examples to whet your appetite:

BRRR	WYNN	THYMY	MENSCH
FYRD	YMPT	VOZHD	PLONGD
HWYL	CHYND	BORSCH	SHTETL
MYTH	GHYLL	DIRNDL	SPRONG
RYND	MYRRH	FRATCH	TWIGHT
TRYP	SYNCH	KLEPHT	WRIGHT

As ever, fuller lists appear in *Official Scrabble Lists*.

6-plus-1 Combinations

You have the letters AEINST on your rack, plus a blank. What are the possible seven-letter words that you can make? There are the easy ones, such as DETAINS and NASTIER; and there are the less obvious ones, such as TAJINES and WANTIES. There are scores of others, too. Having spotted one or several seven-letter words on your rack is one thing; whether any of them will go down on the board at a particular point in a game is something else!

6-plus-1 combinations concentrate on finding common groups of six letters, and then listing all the words that can be made by adding a seventh letter. The three most fecund groups of six letters are AEINRT, AEINST and AEIRST. *Official Scrabble Lists* methodically lists the 200 most productive six-letter groups, showing all the words that can be formed by the addition of a seventh letter. Top Scrabble players will know all the seven-letter words formed from the top five or six most productive groups, as well as having extensive knowledge of the other productive groups.

Of course, you don't need to have a blank on your rack for the 6-plus-1 lists to be helpful. Perhaps you just have ADEERST on your rack. Experienced Scrabble players will be able to tell you immediately the seven anagrams, because they all appear on the ADERST-plus-E list. (The anagrams are DEAREST, DERATES, ESTRADE, REASTED, SEDATER, STEARED and TASERED.)

Pick off a few of the most productive lists from *Official*

Scrabble Lists. Try to learn some or all of the words that can be made by adding a seventh letter. Of course, many of the words will be familiar, everyday words, so you won't need to learn those. And, of course, it doesn't really matter if you only learn 90% of the words on a particular 6-plus-1 list. Knowing 90% of them is better than only 10%!

6-plus-2 Combinations

Perhaps your only chance for making a bonus play is to use your seven tiles in combination with a floating letter already on the board. Maybe one of the tiles on your rack is a blank. A blank plus various different floating letters can really test a Scrabble player's capabilities!

If you want to excel at Scrabble, you will need to grapple with the 6-plus-2 lists as well as the 6-plus-1 lists. 6-plus-2 lists give numerous productive six-letter groups, and then indicate what words can be made by addition of two further letters. The most productive group on these lists is AEINRT. Add AB to get RABATINE; or AC to get CARINATE; or CX to get XERANTIC; and so on.

Suppose you have AEIPRS and a blank on your rack, and that on the board the letters M, U and V are floating. Checking the 6-plus-2 lists will reveal the possibilities to be as follows, with the less ordinary words highlighted:

EMPAIRES	PRIMATES	SWAMPIER
EPIGRAMS	PRIVATES	**UNPRAISE**
IMPEARLS	**RAMPIKES**	**UPRAISED**
IMPRESAS	**RAMPIRES**	**UPRAISES**
LEMPIRAS	**SAMPHIRE**	VAMPIRES
PARVISES	**SAMPIRES**	VAPORISE
PREVAILS	SERAPHIM	**VESPIARY**
PRIMAGES	**SPAMMIER**	

Whether any of these will go down on the board will depend on the constraints imposed by the positions of the floating letters.

If you feel unable to learn and retain vast swathes of words from the 6-plus-2 lists, even cursory examination of the lists in *Official Scrabble Lists* might result in a few of them sticking in your memory.

Knowing Non-words

You may feel that it will be difficult enough to learn allowable words, without having to learn several 'non-words'. What are these non-words? Time and time again, you will get a combination of letters on your rack that looks as if it really ought to make a word, yet doesn't. If you can learn to spot these non-words, you may save yourself much wasted searching during the course of actual games.

The best-known example of a non-word is IRELAND. The letters ADEILNR do not make an allowable seven-letter word. Here are some other examples of non-words which occur with annoying frequency:

CHAINER	INACTED	LATERON	LONGIER	PEATING
REIGATE	SEALION	SONARED	TAILEND	UNIGATE

Of course, in attempting to learn non-words, you must take care not to confuse them with allowable words!

8

Playing with Letters

Introduction
Although word knowledge and the ability to assess the value of a particular board layout at Scrabble are important, so too is dexterity with letters. You will need to hone your mental agility, so that you can quickly see words from different seven-letter combinations. In this chapter, you will be introduced to the delights of mentally manipulating car registrations and postcodes.

Car Registrations
British car registrations are particularly useful when it comes to looking for seven-letter words. First of all, you have to recognize that the 10 digits can all be converted to letters as follows:

    0   O
    1   I
    2   Z
    3   E (think of the E as a mirror image of the 3)
    4   A (think of the 4 as a badly formed A)
    5   S
    6   G
    7   T (think of the 7 as a sloppily written T)
    8   B
    9   G (think of the 9 as a lower-case G – thus, g)

Most British car registrations are composed of seven characters. For a given registration, convert the digits to letters, using the above equivalents. If the registration only has six characters, consider the seventh letter to be a Scrabble blank. If the registration has less than six characters, or if the registration has more of a particular letter than the standard Scrabble distribution allows, then discard that registration and move on to another one. Now try these. What words can you find from these registrations? Suggested solutions are in Chapter 10.

RHC	10S	F161	NFR
GAA	731T	G714	SRU
ORU	651V	H135	DRO
ANN	196W	J437	MYS
HNP	130X	K511	NPH
RHN	503Y	L230	USN
A700	NMF	M175	SUH
B493	YGR	N734	UVR
C639	DUH	P707	SUU
D439	RVA	R903	UHC
E508	ULP	S143	TNR

If the task of converting numbers into letters and juggling the letters to look for seven-letter anagrams is too much for you, perhaps you should play one of the simpler games with car registrations. Depending on how much mental exercise you want, you can work with all four letters (including the year prefix or suffix) or just the three letters (excluding the year identifier). If a group of three or four letters has more of a particular letter than in a standard Scrabble set, discard that registration and move on to the next one. With the chosen three or four letters, you must think of the shortest allowable Scrabble word which uses those letters.

Using the car registrations above, but omitting the numbers now, these are the groups to play with:

RHC-S	A-NMF	F-NFR	M-SUH
GAA-T	B-YGR	G-SRU	N-UVR
ORU-V	C-DUH	H-DRO	P-SUU
ANN-W	D-RVA	J-MYS	R-UHC
HNP-X	E-ULP	K-NPH	S-TNR
RHN-Y		L-USN	

Suggested solutions are in Chapter 10.

Another possibility is to use the main three letters only (excluding the year identifier) to search for the shortest allowable Scrabble word that uses the letters in the same order as they appear in the registration. The groups to play with now are:

RHC	NFR	NMF	SUH
GAA	SRU	YGR	UVR
ORU	DRO	DUH	SUU
ANN	MYS	RVA	UHC
HNP	NPH	ULP	TNR
RHN	USN		

Again, suggested solutions are in Chapter 10.

Postcodes
Most British postcodes are six characters long, although there
are several which have five or seven characters. As with car
registrations, convert the numbers to letters. Make up any
shortfall to seven letters by addition of a blank. Since most
postcodes are only six characters long, you will find plenty of
scope for manipulating six letters plus a blank. Here are 20 real
postcodes. See what seven-letter words you can find:

CR4 2NG	EC1V 3SR	NW1 0BL	SE21 7AL
E9 6LY	EN5 1NE	RG21 4LE	SM1 4NR
E10 5NP	HA3 5NT	RM8 3ED	SW19 4JS
E15 4DN	IG3 8LL	SE13 7RE	TN13 2SA
E17 6AN	KT3 6NA	SE17 3JT	W13 0RL

Suggested solutions are in Chapter 10.

Beyond Car Registrations and Postcodes
Playing with letters needn't be constrained to car registrations
and postcodes. There are plenty of other sources of inspiration
for letter juggling, any of which will help to hone your
Scrabble skills. For example . . .

In the Kitchen
Just take a look around your kitchen. You may have some of
the following items. See how quickly you can spot the
anagrams which are allowable Scrabble words:

AEROSOL	HARICOT	PEANUTS	TEA BAGS
CARROTS	LOBSTER	RAREBIT	TURNIPS
CUTLETS	NESCAFE	SARDINE	
GELATIN	PARSLEY	SAUSAGE	

Or try these longer ones:

A LOBSTER	GELATINE	PARMESAN
APRICOTS	HP SAUCE +	PEPSI COLA
CROUTONS	a blank	SARDINES
DARIOLES	MINEOLAS	SMARTIES
EASTER EGG	ORIGANES	TAGLIONI

Solutions are in Chapter 10. (By the way, do you know the two anagrams of KITCHEN, both allowed in Scrabble?)

Abbreviations

Abbreviations, of course, aren't allowable in Scrabble games. Even so, they have a use for the Scrabble player. You will come across abbreviations all day and every day – in books, in newspapers, in correspondence, and just about anywhere that the printed word occurs.

A useful exercise is to take the letters of an abbreviation and to think of the shortest allowable Scrabble word which uses all of the letters, probably in combination with other letters. For example, the letters of HGV occur in HAVING; and the letters of FBI occur in FIB. What are the shortest Scrabble words that use the letters of these abbreviations?

AUEW	GNP	LBW	PSV	VHF
AWOL	HRH	MCC	QED	WRVS
BBC	ICBM	NAAFI	RSVP	YMCA
DDT	JCB	PDQ	SHAEF	YWCA
EOKA	KLM	PHD	UMIST	ZANU
GCSE				

Solutions are in Chapter 10.

And So On

You could try finding valid Scrabble words from girls' names; and boys' names; and colours; and names of countries; and names of towns, cities and states; and famous surnames; and so on!

9

Finding out More about Scrabble

If you want to find out more about Scrabble, there are several other publications which are relevant. You can also find out about Scrabble clubs, and whether there is one near you. You can even watch video Scrabble and play computer Scrabble!

Books

The Chambers Dictionary, edited by Catherine Schwarz, published by Chambers Harrap, 1993. As explained in Chapter 3, this is the dictionary most widely used by Scrabble players. It is the basic reference from which *Official Scrabble Words* (OSW) is derived. Serious Scrabble players will need a copy of the dictionary to supplement OSW, especially in adjudging words longer than nine letters.

Official Scrabble Words, Third Edition, published by Chambers, 1994. This is the latest edition of OSW and it is completely in line with the 1993 edition of *The Chambers Dictionary*. The previous edition of OSW has been extensively updated, to reflect the numerous changes in *The Chambers Dictionary*. OSW is the authority used at all national and club tournaments in the UK (the third edition from 1 January 1995).

Official Scrabble Lists (OSL), compiled by Allan Simmons and Darryl Francis, published by Chambers, 1991. The 1991 edition of OSL accurately reflects the word-stock of the second edition of *Official Scrabble Words*. Publication of a revised edition of OSL, in line with the latest edition of OSW, is expected during 1995.

World Championship Scrabble, by Gyles Brandreth and Darryl Francis, published by Chambers, 1992. This is a detailed record of 22 of the games which were played during the 1991 World Scrabble Championship in London, including the three games which decided the Championship. There is rack-by-rack analysis of the plays made by both players, giving real insight into the playing-to-win style.

Magazines
The Association of Premier Scrabble Players (APSP) Newsletter. The APSP exists to promote interest in playing Scrabble in a play-to-win format, to organize competitions, displays and events, and to publish a newsletter relating to the game. Details of the APSP's activities are available from Clive Spate, 36 Longacre, Woodthorpe, Nottingham NG5 4JS. The APSP publishes its newsletter six times a year. This contains details of forthcoming Scrabble tournaments, detailed analysis of various games played at previous tournaments, reader correspondence, and a variety of other Scrabble-related material.

Onwords: The Scrabble Enthusiasts' Magazine, published quarterly by Allan Simmons. **Onwords** is available from Allan Simmons, 1 Woolmer Hill, Haslemere, Surrey GU27 1LT. It contains regular news of Scrabble tournaments, detailed game analyses, puzzles, and readers' letters.

Scrabble Club News is published bi-monthly by Scrabble Clubs (UK), an organization sponsored by J W Spear and Sons PLC. It contains details on the activities of Scrabble clubs across the UK, developments in the Scrabble world and articles of interest to the Scrabble player. For details, write to Scrabble Clubs (UK), Richard House, Enstone Road, Enfield, Middlesex EN3 7TB.

Clubs
There are well over 250 Scrabble clubs in the UK. There are clubs from Truro to Inverness. For a free list of them, including contact names, addresses and telephone numbers, you should write to Scrabble Clubs (UK) at the address above or phone 081-805 4848.

Additionally, you may be interested in the Postal Scrabble Club (PSC). Games are played by post. This enables players to play opponents from other parts of the country, and, because there is obvious unrestricted use of the dictionary, helps to improve your Scrabble vocabulary for face-to-face play. The

PSC also publishes a quarterly newsletter. For details, write to Debbie Williams, 3 Oak Close, Moreton, Wirral L46 0UH.

Video Scrabble
Play Better Scrabble is a 90-minute video aimed at the family level player. It includes the basics of the game and many of the secrets of success offered in this book. It is available from most stores selling videos.

Computer Scrabble
U.S. Gold Scrabble is the home computer version of the game. Available from most stores selling computer games, this version of the game can be loaded on to your pc. You will be able to play the computer at 12 levels of expertise, or you can watch the computer play itself. When playing at its highest level of expertise, **U.S. Gold Scrabble** is very impressive, and only occasionally will it be beaten by a human opponent. **U.S. Gold Scrabble** uses the vocabulary of OSW. If you really want to practise your playing skills and word knowledge, the pc version of the game provides endless opportunity for playing game after game!

10

Solutions and Suggestions

You were asked to calculate the scores for ARTICHOKES, RESONATE and EARTHMOVERS (see Figures 36-38).

The ARTICH*OKES (the H* was a blank tile) move scored 151 points, made up as follows:

ARTICHOKES 48
MARCH 12
HITCH 9
TANGO 7
KIN 7
ERE 3
DOSE 15
7-letter bonus 50

Total score 151

The RE*SONATE (the E* was a blank tile) move scored 129 points, made up as follows:

RESONATE 24
MATER 21
PARE 5
CATERS 8
MA 4
SKIT 8
ATE 9
7-letter bonus 50

Total score 129

(Note that if the blank is used to represent the second E of RESONATE instead of the first one, then the total score reduces to 127 points.)

The EARTHMOVERS move scored 135 points, made up as follows:

EARTHMOVERS 92
ELATE 10
HOBOES 15
ELICIT 16
RE 2

Total score 135

Car Registrations
CHORIST, CHRISOM, HEROICS, ORCHIDS and OSTRICH, plus several less common words; AGITATE; VIGOURS; GNAWING; PHOENIX; NOSHERY; FOOTMAN; BEGGARY; CHUGGED; RAVAGED; PUEBLOS; GRIFFIN; GUITARS; RHODIES; MAJESTY; KINSHIP and PINKISH; ZONULES; ISTHMUS; VAUNTER; OUTPUTS; COUGHER; you should know *all* the AEINRST anagrams by now!

Using 3 letters:
ARCH; AGA; OUR; NAN; PHON; HORN; FOMENT; GREY; THUD; VARY; PLUS; FERN; SUR; ROD; YAMS; PHON; SUN; BUSH; URVA; UTUS; CHUM; RANT.

Using 4 letters:
CRASH; AGATE; DEVOUR; WANNA; SPHINX; HORNY; INFAMY; CYBORG; DUCHY; RAVED; PULE; NIFFER; RUGS; HYDRO; PYJAMAS; KINSHIP; NULLS; MUSH; NERVOUS; SUNUP; LURCH; RANTS.

Using 3 letters, in order:
RHODIC; GALA; TORUS; ANN; HENPECK; RHINO; INDEMNIFY; PYGARG; DUSH; URVA; GULP; INFER; SCRUB; DROP; MAYS; NEPHEW; USING; SUCH; QUIVER; SUNUP; FUTHORC; TENOR.

Postcodes
CRAZING; GEOLOGY; PEONIES; SARDINE; SEATING; SERVICE; PENNIES; CHASTEN; BELLING; TANKAGE; BLOWING; GLAZIER; UMBERED; EERIEST; JETTIES; LAZIEST; MARTINS; JIGSAWS; ZANIEST; BLOWIER. There are alternative solutions to some of these.

In the Kitchen

ROSEOLA; TROCARS; SCUTTLE; ATINGLE; CHARIOT; BOLSTER; ENFACES; PLAYERS; PESAUNT; ARBITER; SANDIER; ASSUAGE; ATABEGS; UNSTRIP. There are alternative solutions to some of these.

BLOATERS; PISCATOR; OUTSCORN; SOREDIAL; SEGREGATE; GALENITE; PAUNCHES (and also CAPUCHES, CHAPEAUS, CUPHEADS and PURCHASE); SEMOLINA (a superb two-way food example!); ORGANISE; SPEARMAN; EPISCOPAL; ARIDNESS; ASTERISM; INTAGLIO. There are alternative solutions to some of these.

CHETNIK and THICKEN.

Abbreviations

WAULED; LOWAN; COBB; DATED; ATOKE; CLEGS; PANG; HARSH; CLIMB; OBJECT; MILK; BOWL; COMIC; FARINA; PIQUED; HYPED; SPIV; QUOTED; PERVS; FASHES; SUMMIT; FEVERISH; WAVERS; CAMPY; WACKY; ZUPAN.